The Market as an Economic Process

The Market as an Economic Process

Ludwig M. Lachmann

Basil Blackwell

Copyright©Ludwig M. Lachmann 1986

First published 1986

Basil Blackwell Ltd
108 Cowley Road, Oxford OX4 1JF, UK

Basil Blackwell Inc.
432 Park Avenue South, Suite 1503,
New York, NY 10016, USA

British Library Cataloguing in Publication Data

Lachmann, Ludwig, M.
The market as an economic process.
1. Supply and demand
I. Title
338.5   HB201

ISBN 0-631-14871-X

Library of Congress Cataloging in Publication Data

Lachmann, Ludwig M.
The market as an economic process.
Bibliography: p.
Includes index.
1. Capitalism.   I. Title.
HB501.L225 1986   330.12′2   85-29653

ISBN 0-631-14871-X

Phototypeset by Dobbie Typesetting Service, Plymouth, Devon
Printed in Great Britain by Page Bros, Norwich

To M.L.

Contents

Preface

For some years now the body of thought commonly referred to as
'Austrian Economics' has witnessed a remarkable revival of its fortunes
which before that time had been at a rather low ebb. This book has
been conceived and written as a contribution towards this revival. The
performance of such a task calls for a word of explanation.

It is hardly to be denied that economic thought is today in a state
of crisis. Writing the book in such a climate of opinion I could hardly
ignore the bearing it might have on the Austrian revival, its causes and
direction. Moreover, a number of other schools of thought have
appeared and staked their claims. We have what in the current jargon
is called a 'competition of paradigms'.

For Austrian economists the third quarter of this century was a bad
time. To those who lived through them these were years in the
wilderness. It is often thought that this eclipse of Austrian fortunes
was brought about by the 'Keynesian revolution', but in fact this was
only one of the misfortunes that befell Austrian economics in the 1930s,
a decade of calamity. The promise of an Austrian theory of the trade
cycle, which might also serve to explain the severity of the Great
Depression, a feature of the early 1930s that provided the background
for Professor Hayek's successful appearance on the London scene,
soon proved deceptive. Three giants – Keynes, Knight and Sraffa –
turned against the hapless Austrians who, in the middle of that black
decade, thus had to do battle on three fronts. Naturally it proved a
task beyond their strength.

Under the leadership of Menger the Austrian school arose in the
1870s in the course of the 'subjectivist revolution', the struggle against

the classical labour theory of value. Its style of thought has been marked by its origin ever since. It is therefore hardly surprising that the Austrian revival of recent years brought forth a commitment to radical subjectivism, extended now from the subjectivism of utility, a traditional feature, to the subjectivism of expectations and of the interpretation of current events. One of the first tasks to be faced here was to build bridges to types of subjectivism of different origin and hue, such as that embodied in Professor Shackle's great work. The central idea of this book is the market regarded as an economic process, that is, an ongoing process, impelled by the diversity of aims and resources and the divergence of expectations, ever changing in a world of unexpected change. It is my hope that this idea may also gain some sympathy from those whose inspiration flows from other than Austrian sources.

At the end of their years in the wilderness Austrians had to face some new and unexpected problems. The history of ideas has a tempo of its own. As Ulysses, returning to his Ithaca, found that he could not occupy his house and call it his own again until he had driven Penelope's importunate suitors out of it, so the Austrians on their return from the wilderness found themselves unable to resume their traditions of teaching and discussion without coming to grips with certain ideas, some new, some old, but recently refurbished, that had appeared on the scene during the years of their absence.

It is to be expected that at some stage of the revival new models of Austrian theories, of the market process as of cognate subjects, will be presented. But it seems to me that, before this can be done with any prospect of success, a prior task has to be addressed: a number of fundamental problems germane to the market process, some of Austrian, some of other origin, have to be carefully examined from the perspective of present-day Austrian subjectivism. Accordingly, in the three central chapters of the book problems of capital, money and fixprice markets are examined from this perspective and within the general framework of a theory of the market process. In chapter 4 the long retreat from Böhm-Bawerk's classical objectivism in the theory of capital, which started with Professor Hayek's reply to Knight in 1936, was continued in his *Pure Theory of Capital* of 1941, and to which I endeavoured to give provisional expression in my book *Capital and its Structure* in 1956, reaches a new stage. Where a homogeneous and measurable capital stock does not exist, we must learn to operate with the capital combinations of individual firms that, under the control of one mind or a co-ordinated group of minds, give expression to plans and serve as instruments of action. The daily evaluation of these capital combinations in the stock exchanges of the world provides an opportunity for the display of divergent expectations.

In chapter 5 I draw attention to the existence, in the monetary thought of our century, of a discernible tendency which we might call a 'thrust towards subjectivism', a tendency well attuned to the description of the evolution of the sophisticated modern credit economy. This tendency, by stressing the endogenous nature of the supply of money in our world, implicitly lays emphasis on acts of credit creation and cancellation, while an 'objectivist' theory of money has to draw its inspiration from the existence of a stock of metallic or fiat money.

Chapter 6 deals with fixprice markets, not a traditional Austrian subject, but one which Austrians of the 1980s ignore at their peril. For tracing the course of a market process it matters who is price setter and who price taker. As long as merchants act as price setters, for reasons given in this chapter, prices are likely to be flexible; where they lose this role, it has to be assumed by others but prices may then cease to be flexible. Markets are institutions. Changes in the functions of different classes of agents, such as the one under discussion, have to be seen and explained as institutional changes.

Problems of methodology for Austrian economics are discussed in chapters 2 and 7. In this field a rather striking change for the better has taken place in recent years. Thirty years ago aspiring scientists were expected to conform to the rigid canon of logical empiricism. We were sternly told what we should and must not do. Today, thanks to the decline of positivist methodology, a much more relaxed attitude prevails. Methodological pluralism has come into fashion. It appears to offer some scope for Austrian skills.

In these circumstances it is desirable that Austrians, no less than other economists, make full use of their newly-won freedom. For instance, it is now possible and appropriate to raise once again the problem of the methodological autonomy of economics, and to discuss it in a way that seemed barred to us as long as all disciplines claiming to be scientific were supposed to follow the same path. This whole set of problems, as mentioned above, is examined in chapters 2 and 7. In this context there also arises the problem of the relationship of economics to history and to the other social sciences.

For there exists a relationship between economics and the other theoretical social sciences on the one hand, and historiography on the other, which has no parallel in the case of the theoretical natural sciences, like classical mechanics. Natural scientists owe nothing to historians, while social (including economic) theory, whatever its other tasks, cannot ignore an obligation to provide historians with handy and useful tools, i.e. general schemes that lend themselves to application to the real world.

Economists must learn to surmount the artificial barriers which today separate them from historians as well as students of other social sciences. This is an urgent task made no easier by the circumstance that, since the darkness of the age of the reduced form fell upon us, several generations of economists have grown up who do not even know what they are separated from.

I owe more than I can express in words to my friend, Professor Israel M. Kirzner at New York University, the main architect of the Austrian revival. Needless to say, he bears no responsibility at all for what this book contains. I also am much indebted to my friends Gerald P. O'Driscoll, Mario J. Rizzo and Lawrence H. White, and the other members of the Austrian Colloquium at New York University, as well as to Don Lavoie at George Mason University, to all of whom I presented, year after year, the various chapters, and from whose critical comments on them, and on the state of Austrian economics in general, I have drawn much profit. My friends Mark Addleson and Christopher Torr in Johannesburg have helped me a good deal with their sagacious comments. To all of them I wish to express my sincere thanks.

A German version of the Appendix was published in the *Frankfurter Allgemeine Zeitung* on 24 November 1984. I am obliged to its editors for permission to print the Appendix in this volume.

L. M. Lachmann

1

The Nature and Significance of Market Processes

The time has come for an attempt to assess the consequences, for the direction of the economic thought of our day, of the demise of the general equilibrium paradigm we have witnessed in recent decades.

Evidently what is needed is another paradigm. No doubt it will take some years for suggested substitutes to be presented, elaborated, tested and revised. We see little reason, however, to expect that at the end of such a period of experimentation with new paradigms of the 'economic system', one single paradigm will emerge from the welter of such discussions and command general approval among economists. For in the history of economic thought we find periods of divergence of paradigms as well as periods of convergence. The so-called 'neo-Walrasian paradigm', which was really Pareto's great (posthumous) achievement and held sway during the middle decades of our century, did not win its triumph before 1930. What must seem to us the great age of neoclassical ascendancy, the period from 1890 to 1920, the age of Fisher and Marshall, of Pareto and Wicksell, was in fact a period of divergence during which a variety of fundamental ideas, of whose mutual incongruity some of their exponents were well aware, found expression in a variety of schools of thought. As merely one of them, the school of Lausanne did not emerge triumphant until some years after Pareto's death in 1923. A comprehensive paradigm, un-questioningly accepted by a majority of economic thinkers (and, following them at due distance, by the rest of the profession) in all five continents is not a 'natural', and perhaps not even a very healthy state of affairs.

As events occurring in markets are of necessity taking place in time, it appears that in order to understand what happens in a market economy we need a conceptual framework couched in temporal terms, and that in general markets are best regarded as processes.

This idea is hardly novel. Except in cases of monopoly, market processes are competitive processes. Professor Hayek wrote in 1949, 'Competition is by its nature a dynamic process whose essential characteristics are assumed away by the assumptions underlying static analysis' (Hayek, 1949, p. 94). In the same year, 1949, Mises emphasized

> The market is not a place, a thing, or a collective entity. The market is a process, actuated by the interplay of the actions of the various individuals cooperating under the division of labor. The forces determining the – continually changing – state of the market are the value judgements of these individuals and their actions as directed by these value judgements. The state of the market at any instant is the price structure, i.e. the totality of the exchange ratios as established by the interaction of those eager to buy and those eager to sell . . . The market process is entirely a resultant of human actions. Every market phenomenon can be traced back to definite choices of the members of the market society.
>
> The market process is the adjustment of the individual actions of the various members of the market society to the requirements of mutual cooperation. The market prices tell the producers what to produce, and in what quantity. The market is the focal point to which the activities of the individuals converge. It is the centre from which the activities of the individuals radiate (Mises, 1949), pp. 258–9).

Professor Kirzner assigns to the market process a rather more specific function. He explains that

> Even without changes in the basic data of the market . . . the decisions made in one period of time generate systematic alterations in the corresponding decisions for the succeeding period. Taken over time, this series of systematic changes in the interconnected network of market decisions constitutes the market process.
>
> The market process, then, is set in motion by the results of the initial market ignorance of the participants. The process itself consists of the

systematic plan changes generated by the flow of market information
released by market participation – that is, by the testing of plans in the
market (Kirzner, 1973, p. 10).

In following the line of thought of these eminent thinkers in an
endeavour to adumbrate what we may describe perhaps as an Austrian
theory of the market process, it seems that we have to conceive of the
market economy as a complex network of markets in each of which,
and between which, phenomena that may be described in terms of
processes are occurring.

We are dealing here with a multitude of processes and the modes
of interaction between them. For a number of reasons, some of which
we shall discuss later in this chapter, we must expect to find a good
deal of diversity among them. In all market processes, to be sure, we
find the mutual adjustment of demand and supply taking a prominent
place, but such adjusting action will assume different forms in different
markets, depending *inter alia* on what we shall call *proximity of agents*
and their range of action. Some goods are storable, others are not.
Some inter-market processes involve the mobility of certain types of
capital goods, others do not. To ignore such phenomena causing the
diversity of market processes, where they matter, for the sake of
obtaining a level of abstraction permitting us to speak of *the market
process* would be quite wrong. For to do so would not merely blind
us to the variety of circumstances that may shape market processes
and prevent us from taking due account of the very forces that impel
them and lend them shape. It would actually blunt the Austrian research
effort whose main aim, ever since Menger, has been to *understand*,
and not merely give formal expression to, what men do in markets.

There are, of course, many cases in which such a variety of
circumstances in different market processes does not affect our
understanding of human action in them, cases where they do not
'matter'. In such cases we shall, in later chapters of this book, not
hesitate to use the term *the market process* ourselves. The level of
abstraction we choose must depend on the object of our inquiry: the
less detailed the circumstances surrounding the latter, the higher the
level of abstraction warranted.

In this book we shall view the ongoing market process, the elements
composing it, and its manifold variants from the perspective of
subjectivism, or what Popper has called *methodological individualism*.
We hold that 'the task of social theory is to construct and to analyse

our sociological models carefully in descriptive or nominalist terms, that is to say, *in terms of individuals*, of their attitudes, expectations, relations, etc. – a postulate which may be called "methodological individualism"' (Popper, 1957, p. 136, his italics). We may note here that expectations are explicitly mentioned.

II

No market process has a determinate outcome. It is this property, more than any other, that distinguishes market processes as ongoing processes from those which appear in equilibrium models in which determinism is of the essence of the matter. It was in the course of an attempt to let the magnitudes of prices and quantities appear determinate even in a dynamic world (with 'growth') that neoclassical orthodoxy came to grief. The outcomes of market processes depend on what happens at their various stages and on the order in which events happen. This means in particular that antecedents will influence subsequent events *in so far as acting men attribute significance to them* and that therefore the order in which events happen matters; but this qualification must never be forgotten.

At any moment the actor's mind takes its orientation from (but does not permit its acts to be dictated by) surrounding facts as seen from its own perspective, and in the light of this assessment decides on action, making and carrying out plans marked by the distinction between means and ends. This perspective applies to the future as imagined, as well as to the past as known. Interaction as reflected in market events is always interaction between individual plans. Each stage of a market process reflects a mode of such interaction.

Whether prolonged interaction tends to make the plans of different actors more or less similar, whether it causes them to converge or diverge, is a question we shall have to discuss below, but what men adjust their plans to are not observable events as such, but their own interpretations of them and their changing expectations about them. Time cannot elapse without the state of knowledge changing. The successive stages of market processes do not reflect the effect of a sequence of events on successive individual actions, but that of a sequence of interpretations of past and future upon them.

The course of a market process can be determinate neither *a fronte* nor *a tergo*. To believe the former, that is, that a process will end in a position ascertainable in advance and irrespective of anything that might happen on the path to it, would be to return to the equilibrium paradigm and to embrace one of its major fallacies. To believe the latter possible we would have to regard all action as a 'lagged response' to antecedent events, and this, for the reasons given, we are unable to do. It would be confusing action with reaction.

Successive stages of market processes thus reflect nothing so much as successive modes of re-orientation as the mind of the actor fits means to ends in ever new forms prompted by new forms of knowledge and imagination. Old knowledge becomes obsolete as new knowledge is acquired, and there can be no question of the simple and precise form of relationship between independent and dependent variables in an otherwise constant environment. It is of course the continuously changing environment that compels periodic re-orientation.

In a competitive game there are winners and losers. By the same token, competitive market forces will cause discoordination as well as coordination of agents' plans. In fact they cannot do the latter without doing the former. No agent can enter a market, or extend his range of activity within one by making offers to other agents, without disrupting some market relationship presently existing between them and others. This fact is of course of the very essence of competition.

The effects of such competitive activity on other agents may be relatively mild where competitors find it easy to switch to other lines of trade and only circulating capital is involved, or they may be severe, causing unemployment of labour with special skills, or capital losses on durable and specific capital equipment with possible repercussions on the credit system where financial institutions are involved as creditors. The fact remains that coordination and discoordination go together. Schumpeter epitomized it in his phrase 'the perennial gale of creative destruction'.

So far as is possible within the space of this chapter, we shall in what follows explore the rich variety of circumstances that may give rise to market processes, with due attention to links forged within as well as between markets. One of the advantages we may draw from the abandonment of equilibrium in favour of process analysis lies in the fact that we no longer have to assume constancy of data. In general equilibrium theory we have to assume that 'data' will not change for at least as long as it takes to reach an equilibrium position. In dealing with processes we have no such problem. Once we abandon the mechanistic interpretation of processes as impelled by 'lagged responses' to earlier events, results of events in prior periods do not have to become 'data' for subsequent periods. This is of course due to continuous 'autonomous' reorientation.

The unity of market processes, as distinct from their variety, lies primarily in the fact that, as Menger and Mises taught us, men at all times turn means to the achievement of the ends they pursue. In addition, we shall have to assume that each ongoing market process takes its course in an unchanging institutional environment finding expression *inter alia* in terms of proximity of, and distance between, agents and the range of action of intermediaries. Changes in the institutional environment raise a host of problems we are anxious to eschew at this stage.

III

We have to distinguish between three kinds of market processes, intra-market, inter-market and macroeconomic processes. We shall deal with them in this order.

Intra-market processes

A market is a complex of relationships between consumers and producers, buyers and sellers, borrowers and lenders, etc. The relationship between the two market parties may be one of close proximity, so that they can negotiate directly, as in a country fair, in Böhm-Bawerk's horse market, or in those local produce markets in which farmers bring their produce to town once a week and housewives buy from them. Or the two parties may live at a distance (which need *not* of course be a spatial distance). Then an intermediary, a middleman, is needed to bring them together. Where distance is spatial, the itinerant hawker is an obvious example. In any case, the role of the merchant in market processes emerges as fundamental. With more complex market relationships there may be specialization among merchants, horizontal or vertical. We then have a whole chain of intermediaries inserted between consumers and producers, such as wholesale and retail merchants.

A comprehensive model of the complex of intra-market relationships we find in the famous Book V of Marshall's *Principles* (1920). His angle of vision differed from ours in that he was interested in establishing the conditions in which the intra-market process would lead to an equilibrium position while our aim lies in a different direction.

Naturally enough he stylized market relations so as to make them fit into his equilibrium model, while our purpose, by contrast, is to go back to the market facts in their pristine purity in order to see what light they might throw on the problems of the market process in our sense of the word.

It is now fairly generally agreed that Marshall's partial equilibrium theory presupposes the existence of merchants who, when prices are set by other agents, exploit and thus eliminate price differences in various parts of the market, when no prices are set by others set such prices to buyers and sellers as will enable them to gain by turnover, and who will carry stocks enabling them to benefit from intertemporal price differences. The Marshallian merchant is a smallscale cousin of the Walrasian auctioneer; by contrast to the latter he faces a feasible task. We know that in Marshall's Victorian world such men abounded. No wonder he took their existence for granted.

On the other hand, we have to be more cautious than he was. We know from history that merchants may be eliminated, as has happened to wholesale merchants in a good many markets. The tendency towards the elimination of the middleman where his functions can more economically be exercised by others is of course part and parcel of any market process. Problems may arise, however, where not all the middleman's functions can be taken over by others so that after his disappearance some functions are left unexercised. One of the merchant's functions, in some circumstances, is to set flexible prices. We shall learn in chapter 6 that flexible prices may disappear without him.

The merchant needs a steady and large turnover to keep him in business. Where this condition is not met we may find others taking over his functions on a part-time basis, as estate agents and art dealers often do.

With the full participation of merchants, then, and in the conditions postulated in Marshall's Book V, a market process converging on an equilibrium position may emerge. We have to bear in mind, though, that this is a short-period, partial, stock-and-flow equilibrium. While in this position the market clears, it does not denote a 'state of rest'. That it is partial means that the market is temporarily isolated against influences emanating from other markets.[1] That demand for stock and supply from stock play a part means that our period, whatever length we give it, is not really what Sir John Hicks calls an 'isolated period' and the 'static method', Marshall's method, is, strictly speaking, not applicable, since the holding of stocks must be prompted by expectations of future events. As these expectations and the desired stock magnitudes governed by them necessarily change over time, so does our equilibrium position. The market process, having led to one equilibrium position, will sooner or later have to start again. Here as elsewhere, the notion of time is a major source of our difficulties. Intra-market processes leading to Marshallian partial equilibrium must hold some place in our scheme of thought, but a relatively modest one. We have no right to assume that they are the only ones that exist.

Quite apart from the problem of discoordination discussed above, a situation is possible in which an intra-market process cannot start owing to the absence of the conditions of coordination, even though profitable opportunities are in existence and await exploitation. In 1960 G. B. Richardson presented such a case, though admittedly it concerns capital investment, an activity which lies beyond the narrow confines of Marshall's short-period method:

> Let us then consider an entrepreneur who expects the demand for a particular product to rise and remain, for some considerable time, at this higher level. He will recognize that there has been created, as a result, a 'general profit potential', in the sense that the additional investment of resources in this direction would, up to a certain point, afford profits to those who controlled them. But if he is to believe that there exists, at the same time, a profit opportunity for him in particular, he will have to be assured that the volume of investment undertaken by his competitors will not be so great as to cause a substantial excess of supply over demand at any time during the economic life of the equipment which he has to employ. If the existence of a general profit potential were to call forth an excessive supply response then clearly it would result in losses rather than profits for all concerned (Richardson, 1960, p. 50).

It seems that in such a case the competitive market process stalls. Richardson, it is true, is not dismayed. Two pages on, he tells us, 'And yet, in any actual private enterprise economy, successful adjustment does in fact take place, at least in some industries, for some of the time. The problem, therefore, is to explain how this can happen, and, in particular, how the required information is somehow made available' (ibid., p. 52). No doubt he is right. We have to bear in mind, however, that our problem differs from his. What matters to us is not how it can happen, but how it can happen as part of a competitive market process.

Inter-market processes

At first sight these processes do not appear to present any new problems. There may be no close proximity, but merchants will, as in our former case, create an artificial one. The role of export and import merchants in international trade is an obvious example. Arbitrage between markets is just as common as arbitrage within markets. But, here as elsewhere, first impressions are often deceptive.

Some inter-market processes are generated by markets in disequilibrium when excess demand and supply start to 'spill over' into other markets. This of course is a problem which cannot arise within the orbit of Marshallian analysis, in which markets are conceived as insulated against outside forces. Such market forces account for the transfer of excess pressure between markets. While they assist coordination in those markets in which pressure is thus relieved they, needless to say, discoordinate activities in those on which they have an impact. They are thus both equilibrating and disequilibrating forces.[2]

In Walrasian, as distinct from Marshallian analysis inter-market processes are not so much ignored as subsumed in the equilibrium outcome. Behind the scenes, so to speak, the result of the interplay of these forces is recorded, but the process that led to it vanishes from sight. Here, therefore, only the transition from equilibrium to process analysis enables us to gain insight into their mode of operation and, paradoxically, the likelihood of their ending in equilibrium positions. Only where excess demand emanating from one market meets an excess supply of acceptable substitutes emanating from another could the resulting encounter be regarded as an equilibrating force. Needless to say, such cases are likely to be rare.

It may be held, however, that the excess demand emanating from each market in disequilibrium will 'spill over' into a number of markets for substitutes where it is thus likely to create a weaker disequilibrium in each of them than it helps to relieve in its market of origin.[3] This evidently depends on the prior situation in the markets affected, where there may or may not have been disequilibria before. In any case, it is hard to see why, in a world in which thousands of markets are connected by links however tenuous, inter-market processes should be thought necessarily to converge on positions of equilibrium.

Intertemporal markets provide us with a most interesting instance of inter-market processes. Such markets, either in the form of ordinary forward markets or, in their more sophisticated version of 'contingent futures' markets, have of late come to occupy a prominent place in general equilibrium theory. Here again, our interest lies in the market processes likely to be engendered in such markets themselves rather than in the question whether or not they are likely to converge on equilibrium positions.

In such markets there are two classes of agents whose economic functions are clearly discernable and distinguishable, commonly described as 'hedgers' and speculators. The former wish to 'cover' a position they for other reasons have to take up, for example to protect stock they hold against depreciation through fall in price, or to ascertain their ability to buy future input into production processes under their control. Speculators, however, enter the market to gain from inter-temporal price changes they expect. A market consisting entirely of hedgers on both sides, as buyers and sellers, is not inconceivable, but experience shows such cases to be rare. In general, intertemporal markets cannot exist without speculators willing to bear uncertainty where hedgers wish to be relieved of it, or pitting their expectations against those of other speculators.

The speculator is thus the merchant of intertemporal markets. He provides hedgers with the intertemporal partnership they need, carries stocks forward to where they are most wanted and draws gain from expected price differences. His presence is not, however, required to make prices flexible. Prices would be flexible even in markets entirely composed of hedgers. What distinguishes the speculator from the arbitrageur, another merchant, is his bearing of risk, as he must take an 'open position' while the arbitrageur is able to avoid this by buying and selling at the same time.

The speculator is a merchant in volatile markets. His gains and losses usually exceed those of other merchants. Also, while the exodus of merchants from markets that have become unprofitable is as a rule a slow and gradual process, a speculator's exit may be a sudden and dramatic affair, undermining what is already an unstable market.

Even today the number of intertemporal markets is relatively small, and the number of dates for which transactions on them are possible is limited. Indicative Planning, a system in which producers in various industries are encouraged, under the aegis of a governmental agency, to concert their production plans for a number of years, has been recommended as a substitute for the intertemporal markets that do not exist and are unlikely to come into existence. Within the framework of an over-all plan for the whole economy, steel producers, for example, can feel assured of their sales for a number of years while the automobile industry could enjoy the assurance of a reliable source of supply.

While such projects raise a number of issues with which we are not concerned (but also the problem of the micro-foundations of macro-aggregates which will cross our path soon), we have to remember that our perspective is that of the market process. Situations are possible in which, owing to the absence of requisite institutions, market transactions do not take place even though profitable opportunities exist and the resources to exploit them are available. Richardson's case of the hesitant investor, quoted above, is an obvious example. In such cases we may nurture a hope that the market will, in the end, evolve the requisite institutions the present absence of which has caused such an embarrassing situation, but this may be a slow and gradual process. It would be as rash to assume that all conditions in which institutions requisite to the rise of a market process are absent are necessarily of a permanent character as it would be unwise to emphasize the competitive nature of the market process to the point of excluding from it by definition all mutual agreements about complementary investments that may be concluded within the framework of a system of national planning. Where human action is concerned, the ingenuity of the acting mind is apt to defy definitions too narrow for its comfort, and such definitions are likely to take revenge on their authors.

The root of our difficulty lies in this: in a market, as we saw, all coordinating activity must engender some discoordination of existing relations. Agreements among agents extending over a period of time, if they are to assure each of the continuous availability of services by the other, must preclude disruption by third parties offering better terms to either agent, and are, to this extent, necessarily 'in restraint of trade'. It is to be doubted whether attempts to let a maximum number of agents share in the benefits of the coordination of investment plans without compulsion, whether by means of indicative planning or similar schemes within the framework of a 'national plan', can attain their aim as long as consumers' future decisions remain uncertain and discoordination by them cannot be precluded. When steelmakers and automobile producers agree to expand their capacity by a certain proportion each, they may thus be able to ensure availability of resources. They remain unable to assure one another that these will actually be utilized.

Macroeconomic processes

At a first glance it may seem odd, and out of touch with contemporary fashion, to regard macroeconomic processes, such as multiplier processes of expansion or contraction, as a species of market processes of the kind we have to take an interest in. Nevertheless, the fact remains that these processes *are*, in our terminology, inter-market processes. They reflect a mode of interaction between buyers, sellers and intermediaries, a mode which varies with different agents' interpretation of events. They presuppose the activity of price-setting, stock-holding and turnover-maximizing merchants. They certainly involve the inter-market flow of variable quantities of goods between markets and the occasional 'spillover' of excess demand or supply. What keeps these processes in motion, whatever their starting events or 'causes', is the continuous re-orientation of men to new opportunities, profitable or merely enjoyable, or to the loss of such opportunities which only yesterday were within one's reach and the need to give expression to it in one's expenditure plan.

What makes the description of macroeconomic processes as inter-market processes seem so odd is the simple fact that, by dint of long training and strenuous exercise, we have become so accustomed to look upon such processes as mechanical sequences, capable of fitting into econometric 'models of the economy', that it no longer occurs to us to ask occasionally (let alone realize the need for doing so) what forms of human action lie behind, and are hidden by, the formal entities that figure in these sequences. In other words, as regards the events reflected in them, we are so used to looking at them from one angle of vision that we have quite forgotten that there are others which on occasion need to be adopted. The 'natural' market perspective has thus not merely come to be regarded as the less natural one. A majority of economists today appears to be oblivious of its very existence.

It is now fairly generally agreed that what effect an increase in the quantity of money will have on output and prices will depend *inter alia* on whether the new money enters the market system as spendable income (e.g. paid by government and financed by budget deficit), or by being exchanged against securities in the course of banking operations. When Keynes in the *Treatise* introduced the distinction between the industrial and the financial circulation of money on which the above distinction rests, he in fact established, as we now can see, a distinction between two kinds of market processes.

As soon as we examine the transmission mechanism of the multiplier process from a market process perspective its vaunted determinism vanishes. This model shows an income–expenditure flow diminishing in size as it reaches a sequence of markets. It appears to rest upon the assumption that while this is happening stocks are held constant. In market terms, merchants selling consumption goods react to the increase in their sales by increasing their own purchases correspondingly without allowing their stocks to be affected. In what circumstances is this likely to happen? If merchants hold surplus stocks, that is, stocks regarded to be excessive relative to 'normal' size, they will surely make use of this opportunity to run them down. If, on the other hand, they regard the size of their stocks as 'subnormal', they will raise their prices rather than increase real sales. In the former case the multiplier process comes to an abrupt end, in the latter case the process continues as one of expansion of money incomes but not of real output and employment. The same applies, in reverse, to a multiplier process of contraction. The multiplier model we find in most textbooks mentions neither possibility.

What matters to us is this: a number of possible sequences of events the possibility of which we cannot but notice as soon as we view them from the perspective of market process, vanish from our sight when we look at them from that of usual macroeconomics. These features typically concern the activities of merchants as market intermediaries, but in a wider sense concern all market aspects of such events. The reason for this discrepancy we have to seek of course in the fact that models of macroeconomic processes are designed for the purpose of fitting into econometric models of larger 'systems', such as that of 'the economy', and that these models, in their turn, exist for the purpose of enabling us to make predictions about the world. Everything that does not fit this purpose has to be lopped off. We, on the other hand, in our study of market processes, face no such Procrustean need, and can afford to move at a lower level of abstraction which permits us to explore a wide variety of circumstances.

It is possible that, at this juncture, the reader will expect us, in the light of what we have just said, and from the vantage point thus gained, to comment on the vexed problem of the micro-foundations of macroeconomics. If so, we have to disappoint him. On this problem we have nothing to say.

The market angle of vision we have adopted is not merely not identical with that of orthodox microeconomics. It is far removed from it. While that world is one of reaction to conditions carefully circumscribed, ours is one of spontaneous action and interaction. The sad and implausible tale of the Walrasian auctioneer, who is a merchant of sorts and whose activity, after all, was contrived to resemble real market activity, provides a good illustration of this incommensurability.

Fortunately for us, the discrepancy between market process and macroeconomic process is plain to see. That the course multiplier processes are likely to take in reality need not follow that traced for them by the designers of macroeconomic models is perhaps equally obvious. The reason of course lies in the fact that from everyday experience we are so well acquainted with market phenomena that even when we encounter a highly stylized version of them we know at once 'what is meant' (or at least what should be).

With orthodox microeconomics the matter is rather different. While its subject matter is also drawn from everyday life, the market phenomena here undergo a different process of distillation. Or we might say that the stylization is here bolder, the figures on the painted scenes are less life-like and more bizarre. In any case, the entities appearing in micro and macro-models respectively have undergone different processes of abstraction. Remote from the real world as they are, they have been removed in different directions. We fail to see why one such level of abstraction should be expected to provide 'the foundations' for another.

At any rate, we conclude that macroeconomic processes *are* market processes, in however disfigured a form the bearers of market forces may appear in the model sequences depicting them.

IV

It is sometimes suggested that events taking place during a market process, while not exactly determinate, nevertheless have to be viewed as being subject to a tendency to converge towards a 'centre of gravitation'. A notion such as this had a fairly unambiguous meaning within the framework of classical economics, resting on the distinction between *natural price* and *market price*. For classical economists the natural price of a good was of course equal to its cost of production. It was reasonable to assume that every trader in a market would, as a matter of simple technical knowledge, know the long-run cost of production of the good traded and hence be able to assess at once any deviation of market price from natural price. Such deviation would offer chances of profit which could be duly exploited.

Once marginal utility, however, has come to replace cost of production as the basis of value, knowing market value is no longer a matter of simple technical knowledge existing quite apart from market knowledge, but becomes part of the latter. One now has to assess the mental acts of a multitude of consumers and, in the case of capital goods markets, the expectations of their potential users to form an idea of market value. It seems better not to speak of a 'centre of gravitation'.

At the start of this chapter we traced the notion of market process in the writings of three distinguished Austrian economists. We should not forget, however, that this notion is older than the Austrian school of economic thought. Classical economists in fact conceived of markets as of processes. We may also note that the distinction between intra-market and inter-market process played a prominent part in their teaching. While in the course of the former market prices of goods are brought to approximate their natural level, in the course of the latter capital movements between markets tend to establish a uniform rate of profits. We shall have to examine both to see how much use we can make of them. We shall find that while the classical intra-market process needs widening, the inter-market process needs trimming.

A competitive process taking place within the market for a good consists typically of two phases, and in it the factors of innovation and imitation may be isolated as iterative elements.

Let us assume that somebody invents and markets a new brand of fruit juice. If he is unsuccessful he will, sooner or later, have to withdraw from the market. The knowledge of his failure, however, spreads and will be useful to others who may have contemplated a similar venture: it will tell them what they must not do.

If he succeeds he will of course acquire a temporary monopoly position and be able to reap profits. The spreading knowledge of his success will induce others to compete with him by providing close imitations of his product. Price–cost differences are eroded, and we might think that the market will approach a new competitive (or oligopolistic) equilibrium. But this need not happen. Competitive pressure finding expression in narrower profit margins will probably induce some producers to evade it by varying their products: competition leads to product differentiation. Some of these new product varieties will be more successful than others, the unsuccessful will have to leave the market, the more successful will be imitated or closely followed, and the competitive phase of the process starts again among the successful. Several lessons are to be learnt from our fable.

In the first place, the view, widely held, of product variation as a monopolistic practice perpetrated by wily producers on an unsuspecting public, and incompatible with competition, is quite wrong. On the contrary, we have to learn to see it as forming part and parcel of the competitive market process and, often, an indispensable element of technical progress. Can anybody imagine how the aircraft, gramophones or typewriters of sixty years ago could have evolved into their present types without continuous product variation? Are the particular designs of goods we find at any point of time not the result of market processes?

Secondly, we now can see that the classical notion of market process was too narrow and has to be widened. Market processes consist of two phases succeeding each other in continuous iteration, which we may respectively describe as competition in the narrower sense and product variation. During the first, producers attempt to imitate as closely as possible the product thus far most successful, abandoning unsuccessful lines, and the result is erosion of profits in the erstwhile successful, but during the second each producer tries to evade the pressure on his profit margin by setting out in new directions by means of varying his product. We observe an alternation of two trends, a narrowing and a widening of the range of variety among products on the market. Innovation is followed by competition followed by the secondary innovations of product variation. The process ends in a state of competitive equilibrium only where the innovative faculty manifesting itself in the power to create endless variations of the set of products existing at any moment is exhausted. As each wave of knowledge, generated by innovation, becomes diffused throughout the market it at the same time provides the incentive and the space for new waves. Here the classical concept becomes helpful if we widen its scope.

As a twin element to the notion of a process taking place within the market for a given good, just discussed, classical doctrine presents the notion of an inter-market process in the course of which a uniform rate of profits is established by capital flows from areas of lower to those of higher profitability. It is of course assumed that the inflow of capital into an industry will cause there larger output, but lower prices and a reduction in the rate of profits, while the outflow of capital has the opposite effect. This notion, however, appears to be valid only in rather restricted circumstances and its applicability to a world of unexpected change must remain more than doubtful. We all know today that processes involving disinvestment and investment, as the capital flows here envisaged clearly do, must not be regarded as automatic responses to any observable events but require the making of decisions under circumstances of uncertainty.

This notion of inter-market process is plausible enough for an exchange economy with circulating capital only, in which merchants hold stocks of various commodities and trade by turning them over. Any disparity between rates of profit will then cause a general tendency to 'move into' the most profitable stocks and corresponding price movements will wipe out the disparity.

Complications arise as soon as we allow for the lapse of time and attempt to apply our scheme to a production economy with fixed capital. It now takes a number of years for capital to flow out of a less profitable area. With autonomous changes in demand and continuous change in technology, what was the most profitable area into which to move in the first year may no longer be that in the last year of the exodus. In a world of unexpected change investment is necessarily governed by expectation, not by past results. Equilibrium analysis is hard to apply where the dependent variables of the system take a long time to respond to changes in data occurring frequently. But the strongest objection to the classical notion rests on the fact that a measurable quantity of capital that could flow from one market into another just does not exist. In fact the classical thesis has to assume that, low as profit must be to cause a capital outflow, gross revenues received still are high enough to permit full depreciation to be earned on capital value. Where they are not, owners suffer capital loss and are unable to let their capital flow to greener pastures.

We have to trim the classical notion of inter-market process rather than widen it. As subjectivists we have to emphasize that expectations of capital gains and profits rather than actual profits earned govern such market processes, and that the slower these are the more likely it is that new changes will occur while they are in motion.

The importance of expectations for the course of market processes needs no emphasis. Expectations, and the divergence of those held by different agents at the same time, play a prominent part among the forces that give rise to and lend shape to the multitude and variety of market processes. In general, the more durable the goods traded in a market, the more important are expectations for it. In capital goods markets and those for durable consumer goods they matter more than in those for simple consumer goods. In a modern market economy, in which there are markets for permanent assets, such as shares in capital combinations which outlast the individual capital goods forming part of them, expectations matter more in these markets than in those for single capital goods, first or second-hand. Here expectations matter not only because such capital combinations are regarded as sources of income streams extending into an infinite future, but also for another reason often not fully appreciated: while flows of consumer goods end at the consumption stage and stocks of them usually bear some relation to the rate of flow, all permanent assets that have ever been created still are, in principle, at least potentially 'in the market'.[4]

Three consequences of these circumstances stand out. First, it is only in the permanent asset markets mentioned that expectations fully come into their own. The market for cauliflower, largely shaped by tastes and available resources, offers little scope for expectational ingenuity. The markets for aluminium and cargo vessels have more to offer in this regard, but in the Stock Exchanges of the world price formation is almost entirely governed by the 'bullishness and bearishness' of asset holders, actual or potential.

Second, at each price the volume of transactions depends here on the disparity of expectations. With convergent expectations there would be no need for any transactions. Changes in expectations would cause prices to change without any deals taking place. In the real world such markets exist because there is a need for such transactions.

Third, however minute the proportion of total assets traded each day, the price changes resulting are of far-reaching importance in a market economy. They affect all asset holders and their creditors by bestowing capital gains and inflicting capital losses. In such a society the mode of distribution of wealth is changing by the hour – hardly a 'datum'.

V

In the following chapters the notion of market process will be elaborated by applying it to economic phenomena in a number of fields. We shall endeavour to show that by regarding such phenomena as episodes occurring in the course of an ongoing process it is possible to distil meanings from them that appear to elude those who use a more traditional approach, and, at the same time, to elucidate the nature and significance of market processes.

In chapter 2, we attempt to provide the market process with a firm foundation in methodology. Needless to say, this has to conform to the postulate of methodological individualism, or *subjectivism*, which sees in spontaneous human action the mainspring of economic events. Mere model-building serving merely the purpose of simplification in which, together with dozens of unimportant items of detail, the acts of our minds may be abstracted from will not do.

The multitude and variety of market processes seems to us to call for a central concept of a special kind, an *ideal type* to which various actual market processes can be compared in such fashion that the various characters they exhibit permit us to study them in terms of proximity and distance from it. The difference between an ideal type and the models commonly in use consists in that, while in both cases we abstract from a mass of unnecessary detail, in the former we actually *accentuate* the features we wish to study. We may need several ideal types where variety is vast.

In chapter 3 we are concerned with the role of information and knowledge in market processes. In expounding the latter we stressed the need for continuous re-orientation evidently requiring a stream of information all of which becomes obsolete after a time interval which may vary from an after-dinner hour to a generation. What needs emphasis is that information has to be interpreted by active minds, 'signals' decoded without the help of a permanent code book.

In chapters 4 and 5 we come to deal with capital and money. It is of course well known that both are essentially disequilibrating forces, that neither fits into an equilibrium model. Both denote, in Shackle's words, 'protean entities'. By the same token, changes in them are among the major forces that keep market processes in motion.

In chapter 4, after stressing heterogeneity, complementarity and the importance of capital combinations as elements of the capital structure, we make an attempt to detach capital theory from its classical moorings. In the real world men try to make capital gains and avoid losses. Capital values depend on expectations. We endeavour to show why attempts to revive the classical view according to which capital is nothing but the source of profit cannot be accepted.

In chapter 5 our subject is 'Money and the Market Process'. The phenomena of a credit economy call for a subjectivist approach and lend themselves to an interpretative style of thought. We trace the evolution of 'monetary subjectivism' from Pigou via Hicks and Keynes to Friedman, but have to conclude that not all of them are equally steadfast subjectivists.

In chapter 6, 'Markets and the Market', we return to the subject of the multitude and variety of market processes. We reach two main conclusions: first, that different markets, characterized by the encounter of different classes of agents with different interests and functions, will give rise to market processes of various kinds; second, that, while it is obvious that we need a conceptual apparatus offering scope for planning and planned action in order to understand the working of a production economy, we need it no less to understand any other economic activity whatever.

A major revision of the foundations of economic theory with more emphasis on planned action and less emphasis on mere reaction to changing circumstances, such as is usually depicted as movement along given indifference curves, now appears to be called for.

Finally, in chapter 7 we examine the conditions in which the notion of equilibrium will prove useful. At the end of it we discuss the nature of the relationship between economic theory and history.

NOTES

1   His analysis is partial in the more interesting sense that firms are managed by entrepreneurs operating in a short slice of *historical* time – they make decisions under conditions of uncertainty (as distinct from calculable risk). To subject the Marshallian model to a rigorous formulation within a coherent system of general equilibrium would suppress precisely what Marshall wanted short-period analysis for: the study of the choices of a particular entrepreneur, possessed of an historically given productive capacity, and making decisions which may turn out to be wrong, but which nevertheless result in the firm being in equilibrium (given the expectations guiding its conduct) for a short period of time. Such decisions may be inconsistent with the actions (of which the entrepreneur is not aware) being taken by other firms. This is a sort of equilibrium of a rough and ready, *partial* kind and it enabled Marshall to conduct a richly informative analysis of the short-period behaviour of individual agents and of particular markets. It is not at all the timeless, or momentary, *general* equilibrium of neo-Walrasian theory in which all agents make naturally consistent decisions.

   The strength of Marshall's method, mirrored in much of Robinson's work, is that it highlights those partial and ultimately inconsistent equilibria which may be the nearest we can come to depicting certain aspects of real life – the *formation* of short-run relative prices, for example (Gram and Walsh, 1983, pp. 520–21, their italics).

While we are in almost complete agreement with the authors in regard to their interpretation of the real significance of Marshall's work, it seems to us that it might help us to understand his work even better, were we to regard his 'partial analysis' as the first step in an attempt to see the market as a process – as Austrians do.

As regards price formation, moreover, we only can reiterate that in the *Principles* the role of the merchant is presupposed rather than examined.

2 Only as long as we embrace the Walrasian notion of one general equilibrium position can a market force be unequivocally consigned to the equilibrating or disequilibrating variety. Once we adopt Marshall's view (as adumbrated in note 1 above) of a multitude of market equilibria it becomes possible for a market force to belong to both in regard to different equilibria.

3 How to measure disequilibrium raises awkward problems. The monetary magnitude of excess demand or supply has to be related to the size of the market. How the latter is to be measured raises even more difficult problems.

4 There are of course many reasons why prices in some markets fluctuate more than in others. One of them is the ease of 'switching sides' in the market, the ability to turn 'bull' in the afternoon after one has acted as a 'bear' in the morning. For obvious reasons this would be more difficult in the cauliflower market than in the Stock Exchange.

2

The Methodology
of Human Action

I

In this chapter we shall have to ascertain the methodological status of the model of the market process. In espousing it we evidently have to show what problems that would defy other models we hope to solve by means of it. Different models serve different purposes. One might prefer one model to another because 'it yields better predictions'. But in the field of human action at least, where knowledge which prompts all action may change between the date of prediction and the date to which the prediction applies, prediction raises more problems than it serves to resolve.

We hope that our model may be of particular use in helping us grasp the nature of processes that occurred in history and in providing a basis for the comparative study of various such processes. In other words, the fact that our model describes a sequence of events in time may make it a particularly suitable medium for the study of real processes which show the same characteristics. In this way our model may be germane to the issue of *history* versus *equilibrium*, the full significance of which for the methodology of economics is gradually becoming recognized. But before turning to these weighty issues we have to face another task: we have to look at our model from the perspective of the history of economic thought.

From a methodological point of view we may regard the economic thought of the last hundred years as marked by a long drawn-out struggle between two contending forces, *subjectivism* and *formalism*.

While the formalists present models characterized by constant relation-ships between formal entities (even though these are in general supposed to reflect measurable magnitudes), subjectivists see social phenomena as the outcome of human action guided by plans (even though these often fail) and prompted by mental acts. While subjectivist models also of course depict relationships between formal entities these need not, and in a world of changing knowledge cannot, remain constant. Professor Shackle has neatly summed up the subjectivist critique of the methods of formalism:

> Scalar quantification, mechanism, description of the structure and life of economic society in terms of stable mathematical functions and a closed system of accounts have seemed easy and tempting . . . The face of things which has thus been concealed and undervalued consists, among other matters, in the inconstancy of any system whose elements, in fact, are thoughts actual or potential, and not things (Shackle, 1972, p. 361).

Professor Hayek has given it as his view that 'it is probably no exaggeration to say that every important advance in economic theory during the last hundred years was a further step in the consistent application of subjectivism' (Hayek, 1955, p. 31). Naturally we think of marginal utility and expectations, but have to remember that, while the former's victory in the 1870s was swift and dramatic, the introduction of expectations into economic theory was a rather slow and gradual process, and that it took a long time before the incompatibility of expectations and the framework of the static method came to be understood.

The progress of subjectivism not only took place at an uneven pace but also encountered a good deal of resistance. We may briefly distinguish three types of obstacles it met. There was, in the first place, the 'open' resistance which we find in such forms as the recent attempts to revive Ricardian thinking on costs and value, or the endeavour to turn expectations into 'dependent variables' of 'business experience' which, at one time, enjoyed the support of such distinguished figures as Professor Lundberg and Schumpeter. Secondly, within the framework of the general equilibrium model an attempt was made to 'reconcile' subjective wants with 'objective circumstances' by giving them the status of a class of 'data' along with other, 'objective' data, such as 'resources' and technical knowledge. All we need to say about this attempt is that it rests on a confusion between means and ends.

Means (resources) cannot exist independently of the ends they serve, while ends (wants) have no such subservient status. To treat means and ends as 'independent variables' belonging to different 'classes' of data is absurd. They are not *in pari materia*.

An even more sinister development has to be seen, third, in the tendency, noticeable in particular in the products of the textbook industry, to assume 'given tastes' of individuals, that is, an ordered comprehensive preference field for each individual, and to proceed to the solution of economic problems of all kinds, which have thus been surreptitiously turned into merely technical ones, on this slippery basis. As Lord Robbins explained more than four decades ago, 'the problem of technique and the problem of economy are fundamentally different problems. To use Professor Mayer's very elegant way of putting the distinction, the problem of technique arises when there is one end and a multiplicity of means, the problem of economy when both the ends and the means are multiple' (Robbins, 1935, p. 35). Some of the cutting edge of subjectivism was blunted when, by means of the assumption of 'given tastes', some consequences of the fact that, to economic agents, ends to be sought and expectations to be held are ever problematical, were made to vanish into thin air.

As we said above, the introduction of expectations into the central area of economic theory was a slow process. Expectations did not make much of an impact, in Anglo-Saxon economics at least, before the 1930s, the decade of the Great Depression. Though the roots of the problem of expectations in the work of Knight and Schumpeter are evident, to most economists today their introduction is probably associated with the names of Keynes and Myrdal. It is a curious fact that the Austrians, whom we would have expected, as Menger's heirs, to grasp with both hands this golden opportunity to strengthen and expand their heritage of subjectivism, missed their chance and took no prominent part in the discussions of the 1930s. It was left to Professor Shackle, almost single-handedly, to pursue this subject, to wrest it, with admirable verve and consummate skill, from the hands of the formalists and turn it into one of the most effective weapons of subjectivism.

It is readily seen how the model of the market process fits into the brief sketch just drawn. It adds strength to the case for subjectivism by elucidating the nature of contending market forces. It rests on divergent expectations and unexpected change. The former naturally constitute a force congenial to subjectivism. The latter, as we saw earlier, only becomes a regular force where it reflects the incessant exercise of human ingenuity causing daily surprise to competitors and customers alike. There can be no unexpected change which does not upset some plan and does not lead to the revision of some expectation. Formalists can find little comfort in it.

We now have to look at our model from a historical perspective related to, but nevertheless different from, the one just adopted. From Sir John Hicks we have recently learned to distinguish between *plutology*, the science of wealth, of production and distribution, and *catallactics*, the science of exchange (Hicks, 1976a, pp. 212–16). Before 1870 economics was concerned with the 'wealth of nations', that is, the production and distribution of goods. But in the 1870s, partly no doubt as a result of the failure of the classical 'research programme', interest shifted to the manifold ways in which markets function and to the determination of prices.

> Though marginal utility had its difficulties (difficulties of which we in our time have become increasingly aware) it was becoming easier to think of individuals' having given wants, or given utility functions, than to swallow the homogeneous wealth of the Old Political Economy. It was easier to think of the economic system as a system of interrelated markets (Walras) or as an adjustment of means to ends (Menger) than to keep up the fiction of the social product any longer (ibid., p. 214).

In 1956 Joan Robinson, in the opening passage of her *Accumulation of Capital*, gave expression to a similar thought:

> Economic analysis, serving for two centuries to win an understanding of the Nature and Causes of the Wealth of Nations, has been fobbed off with another bride – a Theory of Value . . . Both sets of problems require to be solved, but each has to be tackled separately, ruling the other out by simplifying assumptions. Faced with the choice of which to sacrifice first, economists for the last hundred years have sacrificed dynamic theory in order to discuss relative prices (p. v).

It is obvious that subjectivism is closely linked to catallactics since market phenomena cannot be explained except in terms of individual plans. The relationship between formalism and plutology is perhaps somewhat less obvious. Adam Smith was certainly no formalist though Ricardo was; and only in Mr Sraffa's famous (1960) work did formalistic plutology for once come into its own.

The market process model fits into the framework of catallactic inquiry readily enough. It serves the elucidation of market relationships. In this regard it enjoys a considerable advantage over the general equilibrium model in that it permits us to extend catallactic inquiry to market relationships over time, a problem that has hitherto defied equilibrium analysis. The market process is by its nature a diachronic, while general equilibrium is a synchronic model. At the same time we are now able to see how general equilibrium serves a plutological purpose that proved indispensable for the renaissance of modern plutology in theories of employment and growth: without a set of ascertainable equilibrium prices for every good and service produced we would be unable to reduce the heterogeneous mass of output to that manageable homogeneity without which our modern macro-aggregates make no sense. That this is not usually understood and we actually find the belief widely held that general equilibrium belongs to microeconomics rather than macroeconomics (the modern form of plutology) is probably due to the fact that it originally took shape in the work of Walras and Pareto, two renowned catallactists. We have here merely another instance of the phenomenon that toolmakers in the sphere of the mind have little power over the uses to which their tools are put. Durable tools may well be used for purposes never dreamt of by their creators.

We may also notice here another ironical feature of the situation caused by the rise of modern macroeconomics: While plutologists, classical and modern, are mainly interested in output and employment and naturally prefer production economy models to a model of a pure exchange economy such as general equilibrium, which they often affect to disdain, they nevertheless have to depend on the latter to supply them with a manageable measure of output 'as a whole', a measure no production economy model could provide for them. It is perhaps unnecessary for us to show why in a world of changing knowledge not even Sraffa's 'standard commodity' will serve as such a measure.

Only committed subjectivists (or catallactists) can reject the general equilibrium model with a good conscience.

II

We now have to turn to the methodological issues facing economists today. Even the staunchest adherents of the view that economics is a 'science' and that economists must therefore devote themselves to the search for empirical generalizations of comprehensive character (whether or not we want to speak of 'universal laws') will have to admit today that during the last 250 years the quest has not been successful. Neither the *Tableau Economique* nor the Malthusian law of population, neither the quantity theory nor Keynes's 'law of the declining marginal propensity to consume' has stood the test of time. The consumption functions we know can almost invariably be improved by the addition of further variables. As to quantity theory, half a century ago everybody understood it to refer to the relationship between quantity of money and price level. But today it has undergone a strange metamorphosis: we are told that it refers to the relationship between quantity of money and 'money incomes'. We are all aware that the reason for the change lies in the fact that we are now living in a world in which prices can rise but never fall and in which deflation causes unemployment rather than price declines. But as long as we are not told in what circumstances monetary change would affect prices it is possible to feel that not much is left of the original 'law'.

It is of course possible that future economists will succeed where their predecessors have failed. All inductive generalization is hazardous, and those sturdy souls who never give up hope will always be with us. On the other hand, the lack of success indicated by the record of the quest for broad generalizations, applicable to the future no less than to the past, may be said to suggest that the time has come for economists to cast a searching glance at the methodological tenet that has hitherto served as their main source of inspiration. If 'laws' enabling us to predict future events cannot be found, a major reorientation of the methodology of economics appears to be called for.

Let us suppose, however, that somebody were to present to us a hypothesis which, on the face of it, might serve us as a basis for such a broad empirical generalization. How would we test it? All human action is prompted by knowledge. In order to test our hypothesis it would therefore be necessary to include in the description of the conditions of the situation in which the test is to be performed a description of the state of knowledge of all participants. This, needless to say, would constitute quite a formidable undertaking, but it would not be enough. For in each course of action they pursue, men make use of only part of their stock of knowledge. Thus, even if we were to succeed, say, by means of an examination of some kind (and it goes without saying that an examination can at best test the presence of some knowledge and that no examination can ever be devised to test exhaustively the 'state of knowledge' of a person as a whole) in ascertaining the state of knowledge of all participants in our test, our task would not be accomplished yet. In order to specify the 'test situation' we should have to specify how much of his total knowledge each participant is to utilize in it. It is hard to see how this could ever be done.

The problem of the significance of knowledge for action which we have just encountered will occupy us many times in this book. We have just shown that the implications of its existence are felt when we have to specify the circumstances in which an empirical generalization concerning human action is to be tested, but some of these implications go far beyond that. Indeed, it would hardly be an exaggeration to claim that this problem of the significance of knowledge for action is the main rock on which attempts to establish empirical generalizations concerning action which are to apply to the future no less than to the past are likely to founder.

In seeking to establish a broad generalization of this nature we have to give its assumptions the form of a 'model'. We then face the choice of whether to include or exclude in our model assumptions about the state of knowledge of the agents whose actions we wish to depict. Attempts to exclude them are unlikely to be successful. Even quantity theorists have had to admit of late that the rate of inflation may be affected by inflationary expectations which depend on experience of past inflation. But, as we just saw, even if we succeeded in excluding all reference to knowledge from our model we would still have to face the problem of the significance of knowledge for action at the moment of testing the model, as we then have to specify the state of knowledge of agents in the test situation. There seems to be no escape from our problem.

If, on the other hand, we were to include the state of knowledge in our model we should be even worse off. We should have to introduce it either as a datum or as a dependent variable. As the state of knowledge is ever changing it is hard to see how we could treat it as a datum: it is never 'given' to us for long. But to treat it as a dependent variable would mean to treat processes of thought as though they were predictable. We know that this cannot be done. It thus appears that the problem of the significance of knowledge for action constitutes an insurmountable obstacle to the conception of broad empirical generalizations about human action.

The reason for our discomfiture lies of course in the nature of our thought, its 'footloose' property, its protean character. All knowledge is made up of thoughts. An individual's 'stock' of knowledge is a tissue of thoughts, but its pattern is ever changing. The 'state of knowledge' of a group similarly constitutes a web of individual tissues subject to two kinds of change, interindividual diffusion of knowledge as well as intra-individual change of thought. Hence it is impossible to derive a group's state of expectations from its state of knowledge: expectations are individual thoughts orientated to, but not determined by individual experience. Witnessing the same events may turn one man into a bull, another into a bear. There exists in each group at any moment a division of knowledge, and individual action is always orientated to it, but its mode is ever changing because it is linked to thought.

In these circumstances it is not surprising that knowledge of knowledge presents problems of its own. It means that A's knowledge of B's knowledge, however indispensable to the success of A's action, must always remain problematical in a sense in which A's knowledge of molecules, machines or the human body is not. This is of great practical importance as the world of human interaction is based on division of labour and specialization of knowledge and skills. When we engage somebody to help us in carrying out our plans there are many reasons germane to his knowledge why we may be disappointed: his knowledge may not be up to the tasks which present themselves, or he may not know how to make use of it when opportunities turn up, or he may leave our service because he has learnt of another opportunity, better for him although not for us, to display his talents. We never can prevent anybody from learning of opportunities better than those we can offer him. Needless to say, with an increase in the number of knowers, when it becomes a question of A's knowledge of B's knowledge of C's knowledge our problem becomes compounded. It is the ease with which knowledge can be acquired, or may become obsolete, which is mainly responsible for the *kaleidic* nature of the world of human action.

We now return to our subject, the obstacles in the path of our search for broad empirical generalizations in the sphere of action. We learnt that the significance of knowledge to action is the chief obstacle in our path. Knowledge consists of thoughts which form ever-changing patterns as men come to acquire experience.

To be sure, we all have learnt how to defend ourselves with paper and pen (and nowadays even with computers) against the vanishing of thought patterns useful to us, but there is no way in which we can make others retain thought patterns of a kind desirable to us but not to them. Most of the practical problems involved in the knowledge of knowledge have their roots here.

The economist's knowledge of the knowledge possessed by actors in the real world is but an instance of this kind of problem, and our conclusion fully applies to it. 'Economics, concerned with thoughts and only secondarily with things, the objects of those thoughts, must be as protean as thought itself. To adopt one rigid frame and appeal exclusively to it is bound to be fatal' (Shackle, 1972a, p. 246). The fact that, as we said above, in the real world knowledge requisite to action as a rule involves A's knowledge of B's knowledge of C's knowledge compounds the difficulty for the economist as observer no less than for the agents having to face it in reality. We may remember that a century ago Edgeworth and Walras acknowledged the problem of the interrelationship of knowledge and attempted to avoid, if not to resolve it by the introduction of devices such as 'recontract' or 'the auctioneer', which permit traders to conclude transactions only after they have received full information about all the possibilities the market has to offer them.

We thus face a plain dilemma: if we wish to establish empirical generalizations of a character sufficiently comprehensive to depict 'recurrent patterns of events', to apply to the unknowable future no less than to the irrevocable past, we must abstract from the knowledge possessed by the people engaged in these events, treating them like events in nature. If we deem this too high a price we must look for other pastures.

From the point of view set forth here, trade cycle theory holds an instructive lesson. Here we have a body of analytical thought designed to meet the requirements set out above: to depict a recurrent pattern of events with booms and depressions following each other in ceaseless succession. But can we really believe that agents witnessing these events will learn nothing from them and act in successive cycles in identical fashion? Is it not more likely that their action in each cycle will be affected by the lessons they have learnt from its predecessors, even though, as always happens, different people learn different lessons from the same events? Once we admit that people learn from experience, the cycle cannot be reproduced time after time.

These considerations suggest that it may be better to give up the doubtful quest for a model of *the* business cycle and to regard phenomena such as cyclical fluctuations in output and prices simply as phenomena of history in the explanation of which changes in human knowledge will naturally play a part, with the events of each successive cycle requiring different, though often enough similar, explanations.

Some readers may feel that in doubting whether there is much scope in economics for empirical generalizations of a comprehensive character, applying equally to future and past, we have gone too far. They may remind us that in the Austrian tradition all economic action is embedded in a network of means and ends. In 1932 Lord Robbins defined economics as 'the science which studies human behaviour as a relationship between ends and scarce means which have alternative uses' (1935, p. 16). Mises even attributed *a priori* character to the network of means and ends, and Hayek in 1937 spoke of this part of economics as the 'pure logic of choice'. It is indeed evident that all human activity is purposeful. Why should such a body of thought have to be regarded as incapable of providing a solid basis for empirical generalizations of the kind mentioned?

The answer has to be that our network of means and ends, precisely by virtue of the logical necessity inherent in it, is impotent to engender empirical generalizations. Its truth is purely abstract and formal truth. The means and ends it connects are abstract entities. In the real world the concrete means used and ends sought are ever changing as knowledge changes and what seemed worthwhile yesterday no longer seems so today. We appeal in vain to the logic of means and ends to provide us with support for empirical generalizations of the kind mentioned.

III

Let us now take stock of the position we have reached. Our attempt to produce comprehensive empirical generalizations failed largely owing to the effects of presently unknowable future states of knowledge on action. This in no way implies that generalizations of narrower scope, of less than comprehensive character, might not be within our reach. As the main obstacle to our generalizing effort lies in the unknowable quality of the future, it stands to reason that as soon as we turn our gaze from the future to the knowable past the most formidable stumbling block in our path will disappear. Empirical generalizations about the past are quite possible as past states of knowledge are not unknowable, and hence destructive of generalizations, but knowable in principle and accessible to our patient efforts.

Nor need any such generalizations apply to the whole past. We are able to limit them to certain periods. We shall probably find that for those epochs of the past in which states of knowledge changed rapidly we will want to confine our generalizations to much shorter periods than for the ages of slow change of knowledge, but often we may not wish to adhere to so simple a rule. Changing knowledge in the same epoch may not affect all parts of society in the same way. Our choice will often have to depend on which part of society we are most interested in.

Our conclusion that economists must confine their generalizations to the knowable past will be deplored by all those who see the main task of economics in the making and testing of predictions. Our answer has to be that the social world, unlike the solar system, is impelled by forces as mutable as thoughts and that no Newtonian model fits it. 'Predicted man is less than human, predicting man is more than human. I conclude, in an expression of mere personal conviction, that man in his true humanity can neither predict nor be predicted' (Shackle, 1958, p. 105).

Also, in recent years some of the confident claims made earlier for prediction in economics have been somewhat toned down. As Professor Champernowne put it, 'The economist and econometrian need feel less shame because of the failure of their forecasts than for any confident pretensions to be able to prescribe or forecast at all: and to be fair, it is only the more brash who have displayed any such confidence' (1973, p. 909).

There will be others who will ask what is now to happen to the task of economics to 'trace the unintended consequences of human action' (Hayek, 1955, p. 39). Can we persevere with this task where these consequences lie in the unknowable future? On the other hand, if we do not, what other tasks remain unaffected?

There can be no doubt that in the classical macroeconomics, in what (see above) we have learnt from Sir John Hicks to call *plutology*, the emphasis on tracing the unintended consequences of action has always been strong, in particular where Ricardo and Marx, for example, trace the unintended consequences of the accumulation of capital. Economists have always regarded it as within their professional competence to predict the consequences of a debasement of the coinage or the imposition of a tariff. But it is less obvious that in *catallactics*, the modern microeconomics that grew out of the subjective revolution of the 1870s, the same task may be performed with equal ease. Within the framework of comparative statics of course it is possible to trace the effects of a change of 'data' on prices and quantities, but this is possible only as long as the latter are *equilibrium* prices and quantities. Where this is not the case, in disequilibrium situations, the sequel of any action is more action by others prompted by knowledge. To trace the unintended consequences of action would mean here to trace a sequence not of 'states of nature', but of states of knowledge, an uninviting prospect for the reasons set out above.

Shackle's delineation of the tasks of economic theory is therefore to be preferred: 'Economic theory is about the sources of individual conduct and the consequences of its interaction. It is the intimate fusing together of the two questions, concerning the mode of choice of conduct and the outcome of the combination of many men's choices, that constitutes economics as a distinct body of ideas and a discipline on its own' (Shackle, 1972b, p. 587).

Our view that in the social sciences empirical generalizations are possible only with regard to the past will be opposed by some on the grounds that the past belongs to history and that this field of study has thus already been pre-empted by the historians. But of course a field of study is not constituted by the number and variety of 'things' to be found there, but by the relationships between, and ramifications of, the problems the students of a discipline wish to pursue. What appears to be the same subject matter may be examined from different points of view. Man, for instance, is the subject matter of natural sciences, such as anatomy and physiology, as well as of the humanities. The constitution of the Republic of Venice and the public finances of the Austrian Empire belong to history and are studied by historians, but in so far as they each present a complex of structural relations persisting through time, they offer problems to the constitutional lawyer and the economist.

In grappling with the complex issues of the methodology of the social sciences we must beware of undue simplification. We often hear it said, for instance, that history takes as its object the unique and individual while the analytical social sciences (which Mises called by a new name *praxeology*) have as theirs the general and typical. But this is much too simple a view of the matter. By no means all historians are concerned with the unique and the individual. Even where this appears to be the case, as in biography, the historian of course is compelled by the nature of his subject to concern himself also with the environment of his hero. Otherwise none of his actions would be intelligible to us.

'The Life and Times of X.Y. . . .' is quite an appropriate title. It is equally obvious that in writing the History of the Byzantine Empire or even the chronicle of any war the historian is concerned with a 'pattern of recurrent events' and not with anything we could call individual or unique.

Nor have economic theorists, on the other hand, felt themselves precluded from studying the Great Depression of the 1930s on the grounds that their proper field of study is the general and typical. On the contrary, the events of the 1930s attracted their attention precisely because they were regarded as unique. That economists, having once constructed a model of the Great Depression, were subsequently able to apply it to other, similar events is a different matter.

The simplest way to describe the relationship between the analytical social sciences (praxeology) and the various kinds of history is in terms of the respective parts they play with regard to the production and use of ideal-typical conceptual schemes. Briefly, the former produce and the latter use them. They are used, as it were, as a foil against which to hold 'real events', so as to bring out particular properties of the latter by comparison. In particular, such conceptual schemes permit historians to classify 'events' in terms of the latter's proximity to or distance from them. When historians engage in comparing events that took place over a long period of time (for example, in writing the history of the Roman Empire), and in thus tracing a 'recurrent pattern of events', such conceptual schemes serve as the basis of comparison.

It is tempting to identify such ideal-typical conceptual schemes designed to help us understand the past with the abstract models economic theory has produced in recent years in such profusion, but the temptation must be resisted. No doubt, a model may embody an ideal-typical scheme, and in our view should do so, but in economics today very few theoretical models do. Most of them are abstract, and not ideal-typical schemes.

It is therefore important for us to understand the difference between generic concepts and types. We produce the former purely by means of abstraction. The concept 'horse' is obtained by abstracting from the colours, shapes and other properties of individual horses. A type, by contrast, is produced by accentuating certain properties found either in reality, or in our imagination, even though we also have to abstract from other properties found there. The best known are personal types like the London stockjobber of the Edwardian decade, the Prussian

Lieutenant of the Wilhelminian era, or the Paris *boursier* of the 1860s as depicted by Zola, whom Walras no doubt had in mind. Often types are deliberately produced, for example those commodity types which, by the rules of a commodity market, are to be regarded as 'good delivery' in meeting obligations. Each trader is thus able to determine the value of any real commodity offered to him by comparing it with the 'typical' commodity as laid down in the rules. A type, however constructed for whatever purpose, must bear some relation to an aspect of reality. The relation of course need not, and as a rule will not be that of a mirror image, certainly not in the case of an ideal type, the origin of which may be found in our imagination. Nevertheless a comparison with reality must be possible.

In looking at most of the models that have been devised by economic theorists in the last two decades, on the other hand, we find little endeavour to depict traits of reality and less effort to accentuate them. Most of them are designed to reflect a network of relationships between variables, the parameters of which, one hopes, will find a counterpart in the regression coefficients of statistical time series.[1] These latter here figure as a secondary reality, a surrogate for the primary one, a haven from forces with which one is unable to cope. The formulation of type-concepts, it is true, requires only a few aspects of reality to be accentuated. But the methodology of impotence just sketched, which has come to dominate economics in the last few decades, has inspired its adherents with such a vivid fear of reality that they dare not touch it even at a few points of their own selection.

Nevertheless, theoretical models which are genuine ideal-typical schemes do exist. The model of market equilibrium under perfect competition, much criticized of late and not without justification, offers an instructive example. Here certain features of reality have been accentuated. In modern markets the consumer typically is in the position that, unable to 'higgle and bargain', he has to make his choice at prices he cannot alter. In the model of perfect competition this feature of reality is accentuated by being extended to all producers. In most modern industries producers share, more or less, the same technical knowledge. In the model this feature is reflected in the assumption that 'all face the same production function'. In reality most consumers know enough about the products of some (if not all) producers to make them indifferent between them. In the model this is assumed to hold with respect to all products. We have to remember that, while abstraction from some individual properties is as necessary for the formation of types as it is for that of generic concepts, what distinguishes the former from the latter is that some individual features have to be accentuated.

Finally, we must learn to distinguish between *real type* and *ideal type*, a distinction which, according to Eucken, Weber unfortunately ignored. The former is a type-concept the historian has to use when dealing with masses of events extending over long periods, like 'Emperor' or 'Tribune of the people' in Roman history. Such concepts are directly distilled from historical experience and serve the purpose of enabling us to handle it more easily. The medieval town economy or the Renaissance scholar are obvious examples.

What distinguishes the ideal type, on the other hand, is the fact that it is primarily a figment of our imagination and not a distillate of historical experience. As we said, it is a product of an analytical social science to be used by historians in classifying real events and, we now have to add, real types, in terms of proximity or distance. An ideal type may have identifiable counterparts in reality, but it need not have them and may still be useful. The Victorian merchant bank is a real type, the financial intermediary an ideal type. In constructing an ideal type, what we have to bring to accentuation cannot of course be a feature of reality, as in the case of the real type. What we have to accentuate here may be a figment of our imagination, but it must be possible to compare reality with it.

There obviously can be no universal recipe for the construction of ideal types. Let us remember that they serve the purpose of helping us to understand the past, to make relations between events, in particular sequences of events, *intelligible* to us by providing, as it were, fixed points around which real events can be located in terms of proximity and distance. It follows that the usefulness of an ideal type depends on the events we want to study. Outside a credit system of some degree of sophistication the financial intermediary would be pretty pointless as an ideal type.

Where, however, we have to deal with long periods of time and masses of events, direct comparison between ideal type and events may become impossible. It is precisely in such cases that the historian has to construct real types in order to cope with his material. Here our ideal types have to be compared directly with the real types, and thus only indirectly with the masses of events for which the real types, as it were, stand proxy. There can be no rules for the construction of either real or ideal types, except that they must 'fit together'.

We saw above that the perfect competition model satisfies the requirements for an ideal type in certain respects. At the same time, however, it is for us not a very good model since it would be hard to compare any actual nineteenth-century textile market with it, even a real type distilled from such markets. Only when we remember that in such markets wholesale merchants actually fixed prices and thus exercised a function the location of which in our model remains indeterminate, does a comparison become possible.

There are, to repeat, no ready recipes for the successful fitting of ideal types to real types, nor to any other real phenomena.

Among our ideal-typical conceptual schemes those that reflect sequences of events will obviously have a prominent place. Here we have to distinguish between sequences which display a pattern of recurrent events and will require a cyclical pattern of the ideal-typical scheme with which they are to be compared, and others where this is not the case. Chains of events in which causal relationships are of somewhat complex character in that events caused by earlier events become themselves causes of later events call for a special *processual* form of the ideal-typical scheme.

The history of thought has shown that there is a standing temptation to which those who wish to compare theory with history by the use of ideal-typical schemes are apt to succumb, in particular where sequences of events are concerned. The danger lies in forgetting that these schemes are by their nature contrivances of our minds designed to serve as points of comparison for events that have really happened, and in ascribing to them a 'higher' reality which often finds an expression in such words as 'normal' or in the belief that in our scheme we have somehow succeeded in distilling the 'essence' of history while real events constitute 'deviations' from it. All this of course is misuse of ideal types, and we must beware of it. Ideal types and the reality they are to illuminate must not be confused.

In economics, the most flagrant case of misuse of an ideal type is of course that of the notion of general equilibrium discussed at some length in chapter 1. It will now perhaps be clearer why we pleaded for a 'paradigm capable of doing justice to disequilibrating no less than to equilibrating forces, one that will furnish us with a general framework that permits to assess and compare various configurations of these two types of forces', since this is the purpose of an ideal type.

It is also obvious that a self-contained model like the neoclassical is incapable of giving rise to processes other than those of adjustment within the given framework. What, after all, is the vaunted 'stability' for? By the same token, it can be of little use in helping us to understand the courses of events which are the stuff of history. For this purpose we need *processual* ideal types as lines of comparison.

Our notion of the market process is offered as an attempt in this direction.

IV

There will be those who will enquire of us in what way economics can still claim to be a useful science if it abandons prediction of the future and confines itself entirely to the past. Our answer must be that what is to be given up is, in any case, not any successful endeavour of economists, not even a feasible programme, but a mere claim that cannot be sustained in fact or logic. In Professor Champernowne's words quoted above, 'it is only the more brash who have displayed any such confidence.'

On the other hand, there is of course no way in which to gain access to our present, understand its problems and come to grapple with them except through our knowledge of the past. Only knowledge of the past can provide us with points of comparison that make our present problems and vicissitudes intelligible to us. In this respect the real types thrown up by history serve exactly the same purpose as the ideal types do in the interpretation of historical events. As Mises put it,

> There is no such thing as a nonhistorical analysis of the present state of affairs. The examination and description of the present are necessarily an historical account of the past ending with the instant just passed. The description of the present state of politics or of business is inevitably the narration of the events that have brought about the present state. If, in business or in government, a new man takes the helm, his first task is to find out what has been done up to the last minute. The statesman as well as the businessman learns about the present situation from studying the records of the past. (Mises, 1957, pp. 287–8).

This seems an appropriate juncture at which to say a few words about the part institutions are to play in economic thought. For many years there has been, among the groups opposed to neoclassical economics, a school of thought that has come to be known as 'the institutionalists'. Although the members of the school have, in general, conducted their attack on neoclassical orthodoxy on a broad front and touched on many issues quite unrelated to institutions, the name 'institutionalism' has come to stick to this school. As our approach to neoclassical methodology is also critical, it would in any case be necessary to explain the differences between their criticisms and ours. But we have in fact also another, and better, reason for going into the subject. It seems to us that from the methodological position outlined in this chapter, an interesting and instructive perspective on the inadequacy of the neoclassical treatment of institutions may readily be gained.

A general and indiscriminate charge against neoclassical economics of neglect or ignorance of institutions can hardly be sustained. Markets are institutions. So are stylized forms of conduct purporting to describe the actions of large numbers of people, such as the 'life-cycle saving hypothesis' so widely discussed. That a market economy rests on the institutions of property and contract has never been in doubt. At most it might be held that their smooth functioning is too readily taken for granted. And what would the theory of money be without banking and financial institutions?

An 'institutionalist' will probably say that in the models of orthodox theory institutions appear, if at all, in an emasculated form, that we are made to see them in a distorted light with some of their important properties abstracted from them while other, somewhat fictitious, properties are ascribed to them. But all this means is that institutions appear in these models in the shape of ideal types. The institutionalist attack on the neoclassical treatment of institutions is therefore not an attack we can join. Having outlined above the part played by ideal types in the methodology of human action, how can we blame any economist for following our injunction and devising ideal types?

The real case against the neoclassical treatment of institutions does not rest on the fact of the creation of ideal types, it rests on the fact that the creators do not know what to do with them. The types of institutions we find in the models currently in fashion are mostly ill-designed because the designers do not understand how they may, and how they may not be used. We have here a classical example of neoclassical misuse of ideal types prompted by confusion between ideal types and reality. What should serve us as a compass needle to help us take our bearings in a complex world is regarded as a symbolic representation of this world instead. Economists who believe that they can test models built from ideal types, products of their minds, by predicting events in the real world must evidently hope to have contrived them in such fashion that they reflect the 'essence' of reality, if not the whole of it. The features of the world abstracted from do not really matter, while the figments of their imagination accentuated in their schemes are exactly what does matter. These economists fail to see how much more is to be learnt about the phenomena of our world by virtue of their distance from the schemes of our imagination than could ever be learnt from cases of spurious coincidence.

Perhaps the best illustration of what we have said is to be found in the sad tale of what has happened in the last four decades to Edgeworthian recontract and Walrasian *tâtonnement*. From the outset, when Edgeworth and Walras introduced the notions a century ago, it was clear that they represented ideal-typical forms of trading which were introduced to ensure that all transactions take place at equilibrium prices. Their introduction should of course have entailed a research programme for the comparative study of other market forms in relation to our ideal type, real types of such market forms if their number were too large to permit individual comparison. No such programme appeared on the scene.

For almost half a century, however, this and other defects of the Walrasian model did not seem to matter very much as long as the school of Lausanne remained one school of thought among many others. For a long time Marshall's work was much better known than that of Walras, and for Marshall the (largely wholesale) merchant was the equilibrating price maker. Borrowed from the market experience of Victorian Britain, Marshall's merchant was, in our sense, a real type.

In the 1930s the Walrasian model gained ascendancy in its Paretian form. Pareto did not even discuss the equilibrating market mechanism, he took it for granted. No wonder that the generation of economists who learnt their equilibrium economics from him learnt nothing about the problematic nature of the 'auctioneer'. Even in the rapture of the 1930s, however, a few warning voices were raised. Dr (not as yet Sir John) Hicks (1934)[2] and Mr (not as yet Lord) Kaldor (1960a) both stressed on what weak foundations the Walrasian equilibrium price mechanism rests. Keynes, on the other hand, by upbringing a Marshallian rather than a Walrasian and thus perhaps predisposed towards the quest for real types, actually drew Hicks's attention to the fact that on the Paris Bourse Walras' auctioneer has a real counterpart:

For that is the actual method by which the opening price is fixed on the Paris Bourse even today. His footnote suggests that he regarded that as the ideal system of exchange, to which others were approximations. As a matter of fact, this is also the method by which opening prices are fixed on Wall Street (Hicks, 1976b, p. 151, n. 16).

Whether or not we accept Keynes's particular interpretation of what was in Walras' mind, here at least the problem of the relationship between 'the ideal system' and its approximations was clearly raised. But for a long time nobody followed it up. It is perhaps not surprising that economists who had come to regard regression coefficients as their only tenuous link with reality did not find the task inviting.

Today dissatisfaction with the Walrasian 'auctioneer' is widespread. Many attempts to replace him are under way. From what we have said it is perhaps clear that little is to be gained by substituting one ideal type of price-setting mechanism for another until the new ideal type is studied together with real events to be viewed as its approximations.

In publishing the text of Keynes's letter (of 9 December 1934) Sir John Hicks adds, 'It is much to be desired that the methods of trading on organised markets, in different countries and at different times, should be studied systematically.'

We can all endorse this hope even though we are four decades late.

An institution serves different groups of people. Commodity markets serve buyers and sellers, financial markets lenders, borrowers, asset holders and a host of financial agents. Naturally in practice members of each group view the institution from a perspective of their own, a perspective whose outstanding features lend themselves to accentuation when ideal types have to be constructed. It is thus not at all surprising that we find the same institution 'modelled' in different ways in different social theories: the differences probably reflect differences in the perspective from which different classes of agents view it in practice. Disputes about ideal types often boil down to differences in such perspectives. Often they are instructive.

Post-Keynesian economists have complained about the neglect of institutions by their neoclassical opponents. In so far as these complaints are merely an echo of those made by institutionalists and mentioned above, we have nothing to add to what we said, but sometimes the complainants have a stronger case. In the neoclassical schemes markets are as a rule highly stylized as commodity markets, labour markets etc. We should not, however, permit such stylistic artifacts to make us forget that a highly significant difference between the Stock Exchange and the potato market lies in the fact that, except for the potato merchants, in the latter market everybody is either a producer or a consumer, while in the former it is easy to switch sides, between morning and afternoon if required. It is a fact that the neoclassical orthodoxy has, to this day, failed to grasp the consequences of the volatility of asset markets. It does matter which features of reality we accentuate in our schemes, and which we abstract from.

NOTES

1 'One almost has to pinch oneself to keep in mind that it is highly dubious whether the structure of the determination of the variables in the real world approximates the structure of the theoretical models for which this impressive apparatus of thought is designed to provide parameter-estimates' (Champernowne, 1972, pp. 222–3).

2 'Neither Walras nor Pareto faced up to this difficulty; when we do so, it is impossible to avoid the conclusion that the Lausanne equations are of rather less significance than they imagined. The equations of Walras are not by any means a complete solution of the problem of exchange; but they remain a very significant step towards such a solution' (Hicks, 1934, p. 343).

3

Information, Knowledge and the Human Mind

There can be little doubt that, by comparison with the normal pace of diffusion of new ideas in economics, the economics of information has, in recent years, come to the fore at an astonishing speed and is today occupying a prominent place in our discipline.[1]

An Austrian economist might be inclined to see in this development a belated response to the challenge of Hayek's famous article 'Economics and Knowledge', first published in 1937, in which the dissemination of knowledge was described as the most important empirical subject of economics. But a glance at recent literature will soon disabuse him. The style of thought which inspires it is not the Hayekian one.

It is not hard to list a number of problems which, in the last decade or so, have gained importance in economic discussions and appear to demand answers that involve matters of information and knowledge and defy the traditional techniques of analysis.

In the first place, as disenchantment with the 'Walrasian auctioneer' has gained ground and attempts were made in various quarters to put the general equilibrium model on less precarious ground, the question naturally arose how economic agents would come to acquire the knowledge required in business and household formerly provided without cost by the auctioneer. Even in the general equilibrium model of course not all knowledge came from him. Consumers had to know their own tastes and producers the most efficient techniques of turning inputs into outputs. It seems clear, nevertheless, that the demise of the Walrasian auctioneer is bound to lead to the reopening of the whole question how men in a market economy acquire, use, store and replace the knowledge daily required for successful action in market place, workshop and household. All these are typical activities of the human mind and have to be treated as such if we are to understand what is going on. Unfortunately in recent writings this simple rule is more often honoured in the breach than in the observance.

Secondly, questions of information and knowledge are germane to discussions on the merits and demerits of the market economy, in particular as concerns 'market failure'. Where transaction costs are high the market may fail to function, and the costs of obtaining requisite information may rank high among these transaction costs. Moreover, while the practices found in some markets where rival producers inform each other in advance about what they are going to do will hardly appear to us compatible with the notion of competition as rivalry, it cannot be denied that this is often the cheapest and most efficient way of diffusing and acquiring information.

Third, we now have an extensive literature on Search as an economic problem, as an offshoot of that on the economics of information. While to anybody living in our society, with his eyes and ears open and unimpressed by current Chicago fashions, the suggestion that the downward inflexibility of money wage rates may be due to the desire of the unemployed to search for better work opportunities before they consent to a lowering of wage rates will seem grotesque, the idea that economic agents will not necessarily react to changing situations at once, but often prefer to wait and see, retains a good deal of plausibility. What we should learn from it is that changing situations have to be *interpreted* before they are acted upon, and that it as a rule takes time and effort to collect the material required for such interpretation.

Fourth, in the world around us information markets are ubiquitous and the industries supplying them are evidently growing. Economic theorists are as a rule pleased if for once they can feel they have something to say that may be of relevance to the world around them.

Finally, among the forces operating in our field we may discern the influence of a school of communication engineers whose doctrine, mislabelled 'information theory', soon won wide acclaim. Economists, always a little too prone to adopt tools forged in other disciplines without a critical examination of their legitimate uses, always a little reluctant to ask themselves what conceptual instruments the pursuit of their own tasks actually permits and requires, were soon to be heard conversing about 'circuits', 'communication networks' and 'feedback systems'. The impact of mind on mind, however, which all transmission of information reflects, is not readily assimilated to a circuit, and the participants in a feedback system cannot act, but at best react to circumstances constraining them. The usefulness of such tools remains to be tested.

II

Above we said that the demise of the Walrasian auctioneer is bound to lead to the reopening of a number of questions about the acquisition and use of knowledge requisite to human action. There are those who, without actually denying this, appear eager to confine the discussion of these questions to a fairly narrow compass. By contrast, it seems to us that, owing to the fundamental importance of these very questions for our understanding of human action in a world of change, their discussion should be conducted over a broad range and at a level of depth that does justice to the issues at stake.

The former view apparently reflects a desire to save the general equilibrium paradigm from the consequences of the auctioneer's departure with a minimum of discomfort. If, instead of assuming that information is provided by the auctioneer without cost, we assume that agents have to buy it at market-clearing prices in information markets, they will presumably proceed in such a way as to weigh up marginal cost against expected marginal benefit. Thus, it seems, we may hope to find not merely a more 'realistic' substitute for the dubious figure of the auctioneer, but one that fits easily into the general equilibrium framework. No awkward questions about sources and uses of information need be asked or answered. It all happens in the most natural way, in markets well known to all of us from daily experience.

This view, needless to say, rests on a fallacy. The coordinating function of the auctioneer, involving as it does the suspension of time as a dimension of economic action, cannot be replaced by the introduction of more markets without coordinators. Without auctioneers the outcome of market processes in each market, in an information market no less than in any other, depends on the temporal order in which transactions take place. In most cases those who succeed in obtaining information before others will be able to profit from it in later dealings. On the other hand, there is the well-known case of those who hope to benefit from the mistakes of others by refusing to make use of an innovation before it is past its 'teething troubles'. In reality time intervals matter in information no less than in other markets. We have no right to expect the flow of information in any market to be homogeneous over time. This goes to show us how many intriguing questions there are to be discussed.

Our next task thus is to compile a list of fundamental questions germane to information and knowledge, to which we have to seek answers if we are to understand how information markets function and by what forces they are impelled.

In the first place, since information consists of thoughts, how is a commerce of thoughts possible? In information markets the object of trade does not of course consist of thoughts, but of the material basis of thoughts, typically in the form of printed matter, tapes, radio and television waves etc. This fact suggests that the activity of detaching thoughts from the material, of distilling meaning from the flow of information must be a problematic activity we cannot altogether ignore. We shall have more to say about it later on.

To decide what the 'lessons of experience' teach us with regard to any particular practical problem at hand is a notoriously difficult task which becomes no easier where such experience comes to us in the shape of information, paid or unpaid. This is a problem-solving activity. It is easy to make mistakes. Those who speak of the 'decoding of messages' lay claim to the existence of a comprehensive code book no mortal man ever possessed.

Secondly, in information markets we face the anomalous situation that the seller does not give up that which he sells, but retains it and henceforth shares it with the buyer. It is not within any man's power to cede his thoughts to another. This fact creates a unique property of information markets that distinguishes them from the markets for services. While intangibles are traded in both markets, he who is under contract to render services to another cannot, at the same time, render them to himself and thus 'loses an asset'. What would economists think of a market, say for jewels, in which sellers get paid and hand over something to customers without losing it? We have here a market with no limited supply, one in which supply increases with every transaction, and we are apparently unable to speak of any definite 'relationship' between demand and supply.

Thirdly, Austrian economists, committed to expounding Hayek's work of the late 1930s and the 1940s, must be puzzled by the question how knowledge can be both decentralized and diffused. In the competitive market process, as we saw in chapter 1, the diffusion of knowledge plays a significant part. But there must also exist some kind of knowledge refractory to such diffusion, otherwise no knowledge could continue to exist in a state which defies its transfer to others. We are evidently dealing here with two different kinds of knowledge of which one is transferable while the other is not. In other words, we are facing here one aspect of the problem of the heterogeneity of knowledge. There obviously may be other such aspects. One question we have to ask is whether, as in the theory of capital, heterogeneity here also implies complementarity, and if not always, in what circumstances it does so. A related question calling for our attention is what part, if any, the difference between knowledge of general rules and knowledge of particular circumstances plays in this scheme of heterogeneity.

Fourth, we now have to raise the general question as to the precise nature of the relationship between information and knowledge. So far as one can judge, most economists seem inclined to regard it as analogous to that of flows and stocks, a category well known to them. But the stock–flow relationship requires homogeneity. So, if for the reason set out above we feel that we have to distinguish between different kinds of information and knowledge, there may be as many forms of the stock–flow relationship as there are kinds of knowledge.

Another aspect of the intricate problems of the complementarity, and thus heterogeneity, of knowledge, was emphasized by Professor Kirzner in a paper on 'Economics and Error' (1978) in which he pointed out that we would be unable to embark upon any search for information unless we had some conception, however rough, of what to look for and where to look for it. This is as good an example as any for the complementarity of various elements of knowledge. Whether we should regard our knowledge about possible sources of information on what we are interested in as more general or more specific than the knowledge we hope to draw from it, is another intriguing question exhibiting aspects of the heterogeneity of knowledge.

Finally, we cannot but be astonished at the narrow range of problems that has thus far engaged the attention of information economists.

In our society the primary function of the 'media of information' is to supply us with our daily ration of the 'flow of news'. We learn from them about 'events', that is, changes in the 'state of the world'. These media are indispensable to us since without them our existing knowledge of the world around us would soon become out of date. It is of course well known that the task of news editors is a highly selective one.

In the literature of the economics of information we learn little about all this. Agents improve their knowledge by buying information about market opportunities apparently constant in time. The question what happens if the constellation of market opportunities changes while the search is still under way never seems to be asked. The world is stationary, or at least changes only in those parts that are not affected by the search for information.

This interpretation appears to fit the peculiar characteristics of the neoclassical paradigm. There can be no general equilibrium without each agent in individual equilibrium. The latter requires that each agent must have bought all the information he requires *in existing circumstances*. As soon as he begins to take thought of the morrow and to make provision for changing circumstances we are outside the precincts of the neoclassical paradigm.

In our world a permanent market for information with a permanent demand for such services exists because ours is 'a *kaleidic* society, interspersing its moments or intervals of order, assurance and beauty with sudden disintegration and a cascade into a new pattern' (Shackle, 1972, p. 76).

It is in such a society that it pays to be 'up to date with the news', not merely with regard to opportunities in this or that market, but in the general sense of being sufficiently well-informed to be able to revise one's plans in accordance with changing circumstances. It is less a question of improving one's existing knowledge by marginal doses than of monitoring one's total stock of knowledge and replacing those parts that have become obsolete by up to date items.

III

Baffled by the long list of open questions just enumerated, intrigued by the far-reaching implications of many of them, puzzled by the fact that most economists who have devoted their efforts to this new and promising field appear to have neglected them, we have to start at the beginning. But where do we begin?

Phenomena of human action, unlike phenomena of nature, are manifestations of the human mind. Action has a meaning to the agent. We are unable to understand phenomena of human action otherwise than as outward manifestations of human plans which must exist before action is taken and which subsequently guide all action. To understand phenomena of action we therefore have to elucidate those acts of the minds of agents which shape and steer their plans which in turn guide their overt action. In other words, our task as social scientists is primarily an *interpretative* one: we have to elucidate the *meaning* observable human acts have to their respective agents.

All human activity, unless prompted by ingrained habit of mind or guided by routine, is problem-solving. The Economics of Information, it would seem, has to start by elucidating the nature of those problems economic agents endeavour to solve when they acquire, use, store or replace knowledge. What part do these activities play in making, carrying out and revising those plans which guide action? What is the status of knowledge within the means–ends scheme, our indispensable frame of reference for the explanation of action? In trying to find answers to these questions we have to pay close attention to the modes in which the problems involved present themselves to the consciousness of the acting individuals. Problem-solving activity involves interpretation of whatever is 'given' to us with regard to the problem at hand. The task of the economics of information involves interpretation on two levels: while the economist has to interpret observed action in terms of the agents' knowledge as reflected in their plans (their means–end schemes), these agents themselves have to interpret their own daily experience in the same terms. The economist has to reflect on the agents' reflections on what will and what will not fit into their means–ends schemes. He has to interpret changes in knowledge germane to action observed by tracing them back to those acts of the agents' minds by which they lifted out of their stream of experience those particles which might be of use in their practical pursuits.

In what follows we shall use the words *information* and *knowledge* respectively to mean the tradeable material embodiment of a flow of messages, and a compound of thoughts an individual is able to call upon in preparing and planning action at a given point of time. Our distinction between the two terms thus rests in part on the traditional flow–stock dichotomy, but in part also on that between a socially objective entity and a private and subjective compound of thoughts.

We shall take as our prototype of information-using economic agent a business man (most likely a corporate manager) who subscribes to a monthly newsletter and has to interpret what he reads in it in order to benefit from it.[2] He thus enjoys access to a flow of information, but he is also, at each point of time, in possession of a stock of knowledge part of which he may have derived from earlier segments of his information flow, but another part of which probably came to him from other sources. To an experienced market observer the mere witnessing of a train of market events may convey valuable information even though he took no active part in these events. A 'passive spectator' may thus well be an active recipient of information. How do the problems of information and its interpretation, in particular in relation to his stock of knowledge, present themselves to the recipient's mind?

On information markets the objects of trade are segments of information flows which are on offer to anybody. We have a social entity to which the action of individual buyers is orientated. But the buyers, though all acquiring units of the same article, namely, identical segments of the same information flow, have each their own use for it. For each such unit of information has to be *digested* before it can be used in practice. Whole issues of the newsletter may prove useless to our businessman. In others he may find a mine of knowledge. In all cases information received, whether bought in the market or acquired in other ways, for example by personal observation, has to be *interpreted* with regard to its possible use in practice. In many cases no such use can be found. We shall say that in such cases the information received cannot be transformed into useful knowledge. Such interpretation of information is of course an activity. It requires acts of our minds, and each human mind performs it in a different way. One reason for this is obviously that different individuals have at each point of time different stocks of knowledge. Information that fits one man's stock may not fit another's. In general, however, different men's aptitude to make use of information will differ for many reasons other than differences in their stock of knowledge. What needs emphasis is the *subjective* character of all activity concerned with information and knowledge, as contrasted with the necessarily objective nature of the information market.

It might be said that a case in which the market, for obvious reasons, has to supply a standardized product which consumers later on have to adapt to their individual needs by various 'processing' activities can be nothing new to economists. Cooking as an activity by which raw food is turned into ingredients of a nourishing meal comes to mind. An important difference, however; between cooking and the interpretation of information is to be seen in the fact that while there are many recipes a cook might follow, no such ready recipe for turning information into knowledge can exist. This is so because the receipt of information in the shape of a flow is linked to the passage of time which brings change, while dietary patterns change far more slowly than market circumstances and technology in an industrial society. Our businessman, in perusing his newsletter, will find there not merely items that are news to him, but not to other readers, but items that are news to all readers. No medium of information could carry on business for any length of time if it confined itself to helping individual readers to improve their knowledge and unless it brought 'genuine news' of interest to all. But this means that the dissemination of information affects not merely the interindividual pattern of its distribution but also the underlying constellation of knowledge. This is also the reason why the interpretation of information received is a genuine problem-solving activity, while the preparation of meals from raw food hardly ever is. To speak here of the 'decoding of messages' is to forget that the code book changes all the time and that those charged with this task will never have the latest edition at hand.

Enough has been said to suggest that the problem-solving character of the interpretation of information resides in the need to fit particles of the information flow to an existing stock of knowledge. In the simplest case the modification of the latter takes the form of a mere addition to it. Most of the cases we find in the literature, in which the information newly gained concerns as a rule cheaper sources of supply or more profitable market opportunities, appear to fall into this category. But it is readily seen that such single items are less valuable than those which are complementary to an item already known. The case is parallel to one in the theory of capital: investment is the more rewarding the more it is complementary to some existing capital goods. Our understanding of both cases and their implications demands an awareness of the relevance of heterogeneity and its modes as regards the capital stock as well as the stock of knowledge.

We said above that the difference between knowledge of particular circumstances and knowledge of general relations (empirical generalizations) may play a part in the scheme of heterogeneity germane to our purposes. Evidently the latter kind of knowledge is the more valuable since it can be used on a number of occasions. Knowledge of a recipe is more valuable than knowledge of how a particular meal was produced. The question arises whether information about a large number of similar circumstances could ever permit us to draw a general rule from them in such a fashion that we could use this rule, like a recipe, in an as yet undefined number of future cases. While we must steer clear of the dangerous rocks of epistemological problems such as the one of induction (lest we be labelled *inductivists*) this is of course one of the open questions in our field we dare not ignore. Perhaps it will be best to say that information drawn from a large number of similar particular circumstances may, in favourable conditions, enable us to formulate a general hypothesis to be tested by later information. Thus, without violating any Popperian code, we may use information about particular circumstances to enrich that part of our stock of knowledge that contains general rules.

This dichotomy of the two kinds of knowledge is relevant to an important practical problem in our field, namely, the possible obsolescence of the stock of knowledge. As time flows, so does information (under our assumptions) and enhances the stock of knowledge, but existing knowledge may also become out of date. In order to safeguard our knowledge against obsolescence we need some information to monitor it and other information to replace it when obsolete. That one kind of information cannot do both is seen when we consider that information about the loss of a customer will not provide us with a new one. Time is thus to us more than the dimension of the flow of information.

Knowledge of concrete circumstances is more often likely to be affected by obsolescence than the presumably more durable truth enshrined in generalizations. The former will therefore require relatively more information for its upkeep than the latter. (There is an obvious similarity here to the problems of obsolescence of capital stock, with circulating and fixed capital requiring different flows of gross revenue for capital maintenance.) But, on the other hand, the ramifications of obsolescence depend on the degree of complementarity between the part of the stock of knowledge affected by obsolescence and other parts. The invalidity of a general rule must have considerably more far-reaching consequences than that of one particular circumstance.

On the other hand, while the continuing validity of our knowledge of a particular circumstance is, in principle at least, easily tested, given the accessibility of reliable information, the question of how much evidence it takes to shake our belief in an empirical generalization is a notoriously difficult one. Yet it is the part of our stock of knowledge containing such generalizations that is the most valuable and the sudden obsolescence of it is bound to have the most far-reaching consequences.

There is one aspect of this problem in particular which, as students of human action, we dare not ignore. Knowledge informs plans, and plans guide action. Plans are comprehensive means–ends schemes. The means which figure in them must not merely denote resources actually available to the agent; they must, to his knowledge, be adequate means to achieve his ends. When some of them become inadequate, the plan may have to be revised. The need for such revision thus depends on the state of the stock of knowledge which, in its turn, is continuously transformed by the flow of information. As it is clearly impossible to revise the plan as often as information possibly relevant to it is received, decisions about plan revision have to be made at intervals whenever the stock of knowledge that prompted the original version of the plan appears to have undergone enough transformation to warrant it. By what criteria do agents decide when exactly this moment has come?

Professor L. A. Boland, in a noteworthy paper in which he takes up the set of problems centring in 'Economics and knowledge' 41 years after Hayek and examines them from a Popperian perspective, has made the suggestion that how soon an agent will deem his experience (in our terminology, the transformation of his stock of knowledge) to warrant a plan revision depends on the school of epistemology to which he belongs:

> A conventionalist about knowledge might find it possible to deflect such empirical criticism by some form of approximationism . . . For example, he might say that the evidence of a counterexample (an error) is not really contrary to his theory of the world, because that theory is probabilistic and thus allows a few counterexamples provided they are not too numerous . . . Or he might say that only when the error continues to happen would one be pushed to consider changing one view of the world (one must not 'jump to conclusions'). Thus a conventionalist may be slow to react to unintended consequences. On the other hand an 'instrumentalist' (such as a follower of Friedman's methodology) who knowingly accepts false assumptions may never change . . .
>
> Alternatively, someone with a 'scepticist' theory of knowledge may always be looking for indications that his knowledge is false and always be ready to modify it (Boland, 1978, p. 256).

We may not be prepared to accept Professor Boland's argument, at least in the form presented. We may wish to ask a number of questions about it. Is the number of epistemological schools to be taken as given for all time? What happens if some agents change allegiance? Is it possible to be a scepticist as regards the knowledge governing one part of a plan and an instrumentalist regarding that governing another? But whatever our attitude, it seems to us that we must all accept Boland's main conclusion, namely that different agents with the same information will revise their plans at different intervals. We are dealing with human action, not mere 'reaction to signals', and it is not a matter of time lags. It is not to be denied that there is a *subjectivism of interpretation* at work here, and that the effects of its various modes are to be perceived in observable phenomena.

IV

This conclusion now has to be related to what we said about subjectivism at the beginning of chapter 2. We shall certainly want to see in the subjectivism of interpretation not merely a correction of an all too crude approach to the economics of information, but a step in the progress of subjectivism and a useful addition to our inventory. But the more tools a craftsman has in his box, the more careful he must be about the proper use of each. We must be careful not to confuse the subjectivism of interpretation with that of expectations.[3] The former relates current information to the stock of knowledge which governs a means–ends scheme embodied in a plan. The latter concerns the unknowable future. It is tempting, but would be misleading, to say that the latter calls upon the creative imagination while the former does not. To interpret the economic consequences inherent in existing and known circumstances of, say, the invention of a new drug also demands some effort of the imagination.

Perhaps the best way of illustrating the difference between our two kinds of subjectivism is to say that the faculty of interpretation is, at the same time, more than the 'alertness' of the arbitrageur to existing price differences which, if one so insists, may be regarded indeed as 'response to signals', and less than that of an innovating entrepreneur who has to imagine what the market for a product at this moment not yet in existence would be like. It is in this last case only that the subjectivism of the decision which prompts his departure into the unknown demands the subjectivism of expectation.

To us, we said, the arrival of the subjectivism of interpretation means more than the addition of a useful piece of inventory. The question arises whether the new arrival will lend impact to a shift in emphasis, noticeable in particular in the work of Mises and Shackle, a shift that has, in characteristic fashion, accompanied the Austrian revival of recent years.

This shift may best perhaps be described as one from subjectivism as the expression of human 'disposition' to subjectivism as a manifestation of spontaneous action. The century since the catallactic revolution has of course seen other changes in subjectivism. The shift from cardinal to ordinal utility and the extension of utility to cost theory in the form of the notion of opportunity cost come readily to mind. In our view, however, the shift mentioned above was of equal significance for the evolution of economic thought in the last century.

For Jevons and Menger human wants, while differing between men, had an almost physiological existence. Menger said that men often commit 'errors' in satisfying their wants and indicated drug addicts as an example. For the new view the objects of action lie in the future. 'Choice is made amongst the invented, subjective creations of thought' and thus provides no criteria of error or truth. In the older view men, impelled by tastes and constrained by obstacles, make choices which are the outcome of the interaction of these forces. Choice is the *result* of the impact of constraints on human dispositions. In the new view choice is not a result of anything, but *a creative act*. For Shackle, 'A man can be supposed to act always in rational response to his circumstances; but those circumstances can, *and must*, be in part the creation of his own mind; must be, because it is impossible for mortal man, in the life-span he is allowed, ever to have eye-witness knowledge of all his objective relevant circumstances' (1972, p. 351).

For Mises, 'Man produces by dint of his reason; he chooses ends and employs means for their attainment. The popular saying according to which economics deals with the material conditions of human life is entirely mistaken. Human action is a manifestation of the mind' (1949, p. 142).

It is true of course that even today the version of the theory of choice we find in most text-books, couched as it is in terms of indifference curves and budget constraints, is committed to the older view. It will be clear, on the other hand, that the subjectivism of interpretation we found to be a necessary ingredient of a theory of information which attempts to do justice to the acts and states of mind of the recipients and users of information in the real world, will be most congenial to the 'new subjectivism'. In fact we may regard it as an expression of the latter and would expect it to lend impact to its force.

An information market may exist even in a society of 'given' techniques and settled tastes. News about the movements of cold fronts may be useful to wine and fruit growers. But it is all too obvious that information comes into its own only in a society in which every day the flow of daily news contains some items of relevance to the plans, contemplated or in actual operation, of business firms, asset holders and financial institutions. What an irony that a piece of theoretical apparatus, like the economics of information, originally devised to cover serious gaps in the neoclassical edifice and render them invisible to the eye of the spectator, should in the end prove most useful in showing us how formidable these gaps really are.

V

The time has come to attempt to forge a link between the conclusions we have reached in this chapter and the notion of the market process set forth in chapter 1.

It is characteristic of this process that at successive dates economic agents meet in markets, each with his own plan that constitutes a coordinated means–ends scheme, and find that these plans are not consistent with each other. The consistency of each individual plan seems warranted by our common experience that unless we are able to bring the various purposes we pursue into a coherent scheme we cannot succeed. But there is no such reason why the plans of different agents should display similar coherence.

The experience of interindividual inconsistency of plans, of the coexistence of market disequilibrium with many individual equilibria, may prompt agents to revise their plans in the direction of convergence. There will thus be 'equilibrating forces' impelling our agents, but there will also be other forces operating.

In the first place, revision of plans in the direction of convergence requires a common diagnosis of the present disequilibrium situation. *Divergence of interpretation* will prevent it. Secondly, convergence requires that agents expect each other to revise their plans in this direction. *Divergence of expectations* may prevent this. Thirdly, it is of course always possible that unexpected change will compel or induce some agents (for example by offering them new opportunities) to abandon their plans and start altogether new ones. We thus see that divergence of interpretation and divergence of expectations each play an important but distinct part in the market process.

The market process, we might say, is kept in motion by unexpected change and divergent expectations. But the divergence of interpretation, we may add, lends the market process shape and direction. Of this we shall give two examples.

As we explained above, expectation and interpretation are different acts of our minds. One concerns the unknowable future, the other the irrevocable, but interpretable past. It is true nevertheless that the latter influences the former and that the formation of expectations always rests on some interpretation of the past, even though changing interpretation need not cause expectation to change while expectation may change without a change in interpretation of the past. In particular, where the flow of time produces new information of possible relevance to future events envisaged in expectations presently held, the latter may, but will not necessarily, be modified. Somebody holding a bull position in sugar may be induced by such information, if not to close his position, at least to alter the price range within which he wishes to hold it. A mild bull may become a fierce one, a strong bear may undergo a weakening of his bearish mind.

Our second example concerns 'learning by doing', the continuous improvement in productivity as engineers and workers come to learn more about what may be done with a given technology. In the view currently in fashion this phenomenon has to be regarded as a 'gradual shift in the production function', a form of 'disembodied' technical progress which requires no new capital investment. In our view, by contrast, our phenomenon is primarily a manifestation of dynamic product differentiation. Once a new machine has been introduced, different people will use it in different ways in order to produce different products, or different varieties of the same product, which have to compete with each other for the same customers. It is the divergence of interpretations of the range of potentialities of the new machine which here lends shape and direction to the market process.

NOTES

1 We may trace interest in these matters to G. B. Richardson's work in the 1950s; see in particular (1959), (1960). A useful survey, though by now probably somewhat out of date, is Rothschild (1973). Telser (1973) well

conveys the authentic flavour of the style of thought that has inspired much of the work in this new discipline. For an interesting extension of its method to macroeconomic themes, see Laidler (1974).

2 We are here exclusively concerned with the demand side of information markets since the object of our study is the variety of uses to which information may be put. A study of the supply side remains desirable.

3 Arrow emphasizes the subjectivism of both, information and expectations, but fails to distinguish between the flow of information and its interpretation. He thus sees a closer link between information and expectations than seems warranted to us.

Each agent ought rationally to base his anticipations on all the information at his disposal and this may include a great many facts and observations not available to others. Indeed it is of the essence of the decentralized economic system . . . that this should be so. Thus the anticipations of the different economic agents are not only not based on the same general economic model, but they should in general differ considerably from each other (Arrow, 1978, pp. 164–5).

4

Another Look at the Theory of Capital

I

Whoever, in the present welter of controversy on these matters, wishes to discuss problems of capital has, first of all, to delineate the area of his interest and to indicate the perspective from which he wishes to view it. Otherwise the confusion now reigning may become worse confounded.

For us in this chapter the area of problems that together constitute the field of the theory of capital is still that outlined by Professor Hayek in 1941:

> Our main concern will be to discuss in general terms what type of equipment it will be most profitable to create under various conditions, and how the equipment existing at any moment will be used, rather than to explain the factors which determined the value of a given stock of productive equipment and of the income that will be derived from it (Hayek, 1941, p. 3).

By contrast, in 1963, in his De Vries lecture on 'Capital Theory and the Rate of Return', Professor Solow assigned to 'capital theory' an almost exactly opposite task: 'Thinking about saving and investment . . . has convinced me that the central concept in capital theory should be *the rate of return on investment*. In short, we really want a theory of interest rates, not a theory of capital' (Solow, 1963, p. 16).

It therefore seems best to distinguish between Hayekian *theory of capital* and Solowian *capital theory*. The subject matter of this chapter belongs to the former category. This does not mean that no issues under discussion in the controversies that have surrounded the latter are of any relevance to us, but it does mean that only some of them are germane to the issues we wish to raise. Whether or not the 'rate of profits' is an endogenous variable of the economic system is of no interest to us, but some of the consequences of our inability to measure the stock of capital in disequilibrium are such that we cannot ignore them.

It is readily seen how easily the problems of the Hayekian research programme, investment and use of capital, fit into the perspective of subjectivism. In fact it is hard to see how they could be treated adequately except as problems confronting planning and acting individuals who encounter them, as obstacles or opportunities, in the course of the pursuit of their means–ends schemes. Nevertheless we encounter an awkward problem of interpretation and perspective here. In terms of the Hicksian distinction between plutology and catallactics we introduced early in chapter 2, it is not easy to consign problems of capital investment and use unambiguously to the sphere of catallactics to which, we said, subjectivism is closely linked.

Capital goods are production goods, commodities by means of which further commodities are produced. They belong primarily to the sphere of production, and only secondarily to that of exchange. Moreover, the theory of capital had its formative period in the age of classical plutology, in the work of Ricardo, Mill and Marx. These thinkers imposed the stamp of their minds on the matrix of the new discipline to such an extent that ever since the subject has proved somewhat refractory to the efforts of all those who would fashion it in accordance with the canon of catallactics. A good deal of what is problematical in the work of Böhm-Bawerk has its roots here. Devoted as he was, with one half of his being, to the new creed of Austrian catallactics, with the other half he remained a Ricardian all his life.[1] The notion of time as a measure of capital is essentially a Ricardian notion.

The stock of capital is a heterogeneous aggregate. Most of the real problems of the theory of capital arise from this fact, foremost among them that of the composition of the stock. It first raised its head in Ricardo's famous chapter 'On Machinery', added to the third edition of the *Principles* in 1821, in which he had to admit that changes in the proportions of fixed and circulating capital may have unfortunate economic consequences, albeit in the short run only.

Our problems of capital investment and use are of course closely linked to the mode of composition of the capital stock, as opportunities of investment and use in each period depend on the existing mode and the forms of complementarity it encompasses, while such opportunities will also alter it by the very fact of their being exploited. Our perspective on the problem of composition of the capital stock, however, differs considerably from that of the classical thinkers.

As is by now well known, classical plutology is inspired by a long-term perspective and concerned with the comparison of long-run positions. The composition of the capital stock always matters, to be sure, but one of its modes is paramount for the classical edifice of thought, that is, that which must prevail if there is to be a uniform rate of profits throughout the economic system. *This postulate determines the 'natural' (equilibrium) mode of its composition.* Other modes may exist in the short run, but they 'cannot last', hence we are entitled to ignore them. The movement of capital into the most profitable lines of investment is, if not the only force operating in our system, at least the paramount force. All other forces that might affect the composition of capital are inferior to this one and, if they operate at all, are sure to be overwhelmed by it.

By contrast, we are not concerned with this paramount force which, for the classical plutologists, ultimately shapes the composition of the capital stock. For us the mode of this composition at any time reflects the network of plans, past and present, that is, means–ends schemes involving capital instruments, that have given rise to it. In all such plans of course the desire to maximize the rate of return on the cost of investment as an end pursued will play a major part, but an end pursued is not an end attained. In fact, at any moment the existing mode of composition of the capital stock and the prevailing pattern of its use owe as much to the failed plans of the past as to the hopes of success prompted by which present plans are currently carried out. Buildings in the central business districts of many old cities are a well-known example. The present state of the American railroad system is another. The capital stock in existence always contains 'fossils', items that will not be replaced and would not exist at all had their future fate been correctly foreseen at the date of their investment. Some malinvestment is always inevitable.

In chapter 1 we learnt that these are the rocks on which the notion of a general equilibrium must founder. We showed there why a uniform rate of profit in all industries cannot be achieved, in modern industrial society at least. The reader, we trust, will have no difficulty in seeing why the problem of the composition of the capital stock, when viewed from a catallactic perspective, is an altogether different problem from that envisaged in the classical theory of capital.

In 1932, in what was to be the last attempt for many decades to outline the essence of the Austrian research programme, Hans Mayer contrasted it with equilibrium theories from Cournot to Cassel. He drew a distinction between price theories concerned with finding a consistent set of prices and describing those relations between the elements of the system that must obtain if such a set of prices is to exist, and price theories concerned with explaining how prices are actually formed. He called the former *Preisbestimmungstheorien* (theories of price determination) and the latter *Preisbildungstheorien* (theories of price formation) (Mayer, 1932, pp. 224, 238).

Similarly we might distinguish between the classical theory of *capital determination* concerned with one mode of composition of the capital stock only, that is, that required by the postulate of a uniform rate of profits, and a theory of *capital formation* (in a wider sense than the accumulation of new capital) concerned with the multitude of ways in which the composition of the stock and its pattern of use are shaped by the interaction of plans, past and present, consistent and inconsistent, successful and unsuccessful. Only the latter permits us to view capital problems from a catallactic perspective.

II

The capital stock of society is to us an indispensable notion, but it is not one we can make the fundamental concept of our theory without some misgivings. For such a purpose we need an instrument of thought more congenial to subjectivism and less tainted by its history than the capital stock has become.

The notion of the capital stock had its genesis in plutology as an instrument of mercantilist policy, a weapon in the struggle for power and welfare. If our main aim is to increase the wealth of our nation (in the modern sense of national income) as fast as possible relatively to that of others, rapid accumulation of our capital stock is an obvious imperative. It might even, to some extent, compensate for a certain lack of fertility of our land. (The physiocrats denied this.)

By contrast, if we set out to find a fundamental concept of the theory of capital that is to serve catallactic ends, our first step has to be the disaggregation of this macroeconomic aggregate, the capital stock of society. On the other hand, we must not move too far along the path of disaggregation. Single capital goods by themselves can produce no output. What we need as our fundamental concept is the counterpart, in observable reality, of an element of a plan. If a man wants to acquire the source of an income stream, he needs a combination of capital goods capable of giving rise to an output stream. We suggest accordingly that the notion of *capital combination* be used as our fundamental concept. Each capital combination is handled by a *firm*, acting as our unit agent within the framework of its plan, and embodies the material means within this means–ends scheme. We shall think of it as typically composed of land, buildings, fixed and working capital as well as of sums of money and quantities of financial assets. Households have no capital combinations. Combinations of household implements, however durable, do not fall under our concept.

The composition of a capital combination cannot be chosen at random. Only certain forms of it can produce output streams, only some of these can be profitably produced. Technological and market constraints circumscribe feasible *modes of complementarity* of the various elements. This means that capital goods which do not fit into any capital combination, presently existing or expected to come into being in the future, lose their capital quality and turn into a kind of scrap. (Scrap metal of course is capital for the scrap merchant but its various constituent parts formerly served as capital goods in other capacities.) These facts already provide an indication of the pervasive significance of two kinds of capital problems we shall repeatedly encounter: expectations and the maintenance of capital.

A capital combination is a material manifestation of a production plan, an array of capital goods which gives outward expression to the order of means in the means–ends scheme which underlies and guides planned action. The mode of complementarity which shapes this array is, however, not the only form of complementarity of interest to us. There is also complementarity between capital resources at various stages of production, for example between those employed in mining and in manufacturing industry. This second type of complementarity is not the direct result of planned action, but the indirect result of the interaction between the plans of different firms in the market. These latter plans need not have been consistent from the start, but were then made consistent by market forces. We thus have to distinguish between *plan complementarity*, the complementarity of the capital combination of the firm, and *structural complementarity*, the complementarity of capital resources belonging to different firms trading with each other.

There thus arises before our eyes the problem of *capital structure*, the mode of complementarity between capital goods in different industries and sectors of the economic system, a mode of the composition of the capital stock of society. This of course is the reason why we cannot altogether dispense with the notion of the capital stock and the modes of its composition. It will be readily seen, however, why the purpose it serves in our scheme of thought is entirely different from that it serves in classical theory. While for the latter the magnitude of the stock is a datum of long-run equilibrium and the mode of its composition determined by the requirement of a uniform rate of profits, to us the stock matters as the scene on which interaction between firms with different plans takes place, and its mode of composition matters to us only as the result of such interaction.[2] It is thus always in disequilibrium.

What can we say about the firm's production plan in general and the pattern of use prescribed to its capital combination in it?

We might say of course that the firm will act in such manner as to maximize the present value of its expected future income stream, but such a description of the equilibrium of the firm is of very little use to us. Our task is to examine the various types of action the firm may undertake in order to reach such a position when it is far away from it, not to examine a position in which no such action is needed. Our aim, as we said above, is a theory of capital formation, not a theory of capital determination. In order to understand what happens in the world of action we have to ask how the problems they encounter present themselves to the minds of agents who operate capital combinations, and how they go about solving them. To assume that agents invariably find optimal solutions for the problems confronting them would be to assume away the essential nature of the economic problems of a kaleidic world.

In any real situation the firm is attempting to better its position (in its own perspective) by varying its output, its input or its capital combination. In fact the three invariably go together. It goes without saying that in the real world it will hardly be possible to produce a new good, or vary effectively the character of an existing one, without varying the blend of skills required in the labour force, or the composition of raw material input used. Similarly, any change in the latter or the composition of the labour force is bound to have some effect on output. But it is no less true that there can be hardly any significant change in output or labour or raw material input which does not necessitate a regrouping of the capital combination with or without new investment. The Marshallian teaching that in the short run the capital stock is to be regarded as 'given' is apt to conceal rather than illuminate the important issues at stake here.

In the first place, it can at best refer to quantitative change, but not to changes in the pattern of use of existing capital goods. As long as all capital is regarded as homogeneous, to be sure, quantitative change is all that matters. But in reality capital is heterogeneous and, moreover, the property of heterogeneity germane to economic action is heterogeneity in use, not mere physical heterogeneity. Hence short-run change in the pattern of use of existing capital goods in the form of a reshuffling of capital combinations is ubiquitous. Needless to say, all such action involves transaction cost, but also, expectations. The (subjective) user cost of all capital elements affected by the reshuffle has to be computed.

Secondly, the attempt to justify the neglect of short-run fixed capital change by letting all short-run decisions take the form of decisions about flows of input and output, and thus about working capital, cannot succeed. The well-known case of the Marshallian fish market in which (before the days of refrigeration) no stocks can be held from one market day to the next, and fishermen's output decisions are directly linked to market prices, in what is supposedly a 'pure flow market', is not at all convincing. In reality these fishermen would have to buy bigger boats with complementary equipment (engines, nets etc.) if they wished to exploit the opportunities offered by higher prices. Moreover, they would have to sell their present boats and equipment in the second-hand market for existing capital goods at the same time and probably suffer capital losses in these transactions. It is clear that prices in at least two capital goods markets (for new and old boats), in addition to prices in the stockless fish market, will affect their production decisions, and that the influence of expectations about future prices in a number of markets, not merely the fish market, will be decisive.

Thirdly, this insight into the nature of the relationship between output and capital decisions casts some light on the role of the entrepreneur in the market economy. From what was said above it seems to follow that entrepreneurial decisions in most cases involve decisions about capital investment motivated by expectations. There are, to be sure, cases of pure arbitrage in which the entrepreneur responds to a present profit opportunity and need not invest his capital for more than a few hours. These cases, however, exist within the realm of pure exchange. In a production economy it is hard to see how entrepreneurs can exploit profit opportunities without having to invest their capital for at least a few years and thus running the risk of seeing the opportunity vanish before the capital is amortized. Outside the sphere of pure exchange entrepreneurial action is thus always prompted by expectations. It could be otherwise only in a world that would strain the imagination of the most devoted Keynesian: one with permanent excess capacity in almost all industries that would be made available, at their instant, to aspiring entrepreneurs on the promise of a share in profits. Why such excess capacity, should it ever exist, should be maintained until our hopeful entrepreneurs ask for its use, is a question altogether hard to answer.

III

Firms respond to profit opportunities, as they appear and vanish in a kaleidic world, by input and output changes which affect their capital combinations. That this is so even in the short run and has already to be taken into account at the stage at which firms make production plans and have to decide what prices to charge for their products, is a fact which has been generally acknowledged and has found expression in the notion of *user cost*. Keynes described it as follows:

> User cost constitutes one of the links between the present and the future. For in deciding his scale of production an entrepreneur has to exercise a choice between using up his equipment now and preserving it to be used later on. It is the expected sacrifice of future benefit involved in present use which determines the amount of user cost (Keynes, 1936, pp. 69–70).

User cost is intertemporal opportunity cost, a subjective magnitude.

To Keynes, of course, the introduction of user cost signified a break with the Marshallian tradition that in the short run capital is 'given', hence no element of it except 'extra wear-and-tear of plant' can affect short-run decisions. To us two aspects of user cost matter most.

In the first place, the facts to which this concept lends expression show that there can indeed be no economic change that is 'pure flow' change without affecting any stock. Hence every output change the firm plans must somehow affect its capital combination. Secondly, user cost is an expectational magnitude, it is the expected sacrifice of future benefit involved in present use. Different men hold different expectations about the same future outcome. Hence user cost will differ even between firms that have identical capital combinations. The well-known fact that tenders submitted by different firms for the same order often quote prices that differ widely is no doubt partly due to differences in user cost calculated. In part it will be due to differences in their capital combinations.

From the subjectivist point of view user cost, as intertemporal opportunity cost, is a medium of expression for the individuality of the firm. The composition of its capital combination is another. Managers' attitude towards the unknown future, their optimism and pessimism, boldness and timidity, are reflected in both. User cost, as Keynes explained, 'partly depends on expectations as to the future level of wages' (Keynes, 1936, p. 69, n. 1). He who invests capital for long periods gives hostages to fortune and becomes vulnerable to future wage pressure.[3] Differences in expectations about the likely intensity of such pressure will be reflected in differences in user cost calculated by different firms for identical operations. In the composition of the capital combination, on the other hand, the degree of risk aversion of the firm's managers will find expression in the proportion of precautionary assets held. This is no less true of physical than of financial assets. A firm managed with caution and circumspection as regards the flow of working capital will hold relatively larger stocks of spare parts and other kinds of reserve assets than one in which such qualities are absent. There can be no such thing as a 'representative firm' and none whose capital combination could be regarded as a replica of the 'average' for the respective industry. In a kaleidic world the composition of capital combinations, the mode of plan comple-mentarity, changes as rapidly as the circumstances to which firms have to respond.

Problems of user cost are only a part of the much larger set of problems germane to the *maintenance of capital*. Nowhere else perhaps can the difference between the theory of capital of classical plutology and that of modern catallactics be seen more clearly than in their respective treatment of the facts denoted by this concept. It would hardly be an exaggeration to claim that for classical plutology the maintenance of capital presents no problem at all. It is evidently assumed that no rational capitalist wants to lose the source of his permanent income, and it is inferred that he will therefore have to keep his capital intact. It is taken for granted that in doing so he never faces any insurmountable obstacles. Since the maintenance of his capital is no problem to the individual capitalist, no such problem arises for society either. We have here a macroeconomic generalization resting on microfoundations that are self-evident, a methodological procedure of delightful simplicity. The conclusion is not perhaps surprising if we remember the origins of classical plutology in the practical preoccupations of economic policy in the age of mercantilism. Administrators of such policies had other worries than to teach merchants and manufacturers how not to lose their capital. If anybody's, it was the task of accountants to do that.

The belief that the maintenance of capital is, if anything, an accounting problem or, to put it more precisely, that if a few accounting rules, as easy to grasp as to apply, are followed, there is no serious problem, has died hard. In the countries which suffered serious inflation after the First World War it was shaken by daily business experience. In the Anglo-Saxon world it has lasted right into our age of permanent inflation, although challenged by Professor Hayek in 1935 in *The Maintenance of Capital* and a few years later in his *Pure Theory of Capital* (1941), chapters 22 and 23. Today most accountants and businessmen are, to their cost, conversant with the practical relevance of these problems and, in one way or another, have learnt to cope with them. Only economic theory continues to ignore the existence of problems of the maintenance of capital. This strange denial of the existence of a set of economic problems by most of the practitioners of a discipline ostensibly devoted to their study is no doubt partly due to the continued influence of the ideology of classical plutology sketched above. Other influences, we may presume, have also played their part. Among these we may count the futile endeavour to prop up some of the crumbling walls of the neoclassical edifice by means of a capital theory without capital in the guise of a theory of intertemporal price formation. The market economy, to be sure, contains intertemporal markets. Their study is a perfectly legitimate object of economists as long as it is not confused with the study of problems of capital proper, its use, and its structure.

The aversion of classical plutology to serious discussion of the maintenance of capital and its problems is neatly summed up in the phrase 'Capital replaces itself'.[4] No human effort in this direction seems to be called for. This, as we shall see, is not a matter of simple neglect or lack of diligence. For classical economics there are some important issues at stake here. The elegant solutions to some famous classical problems may become open to question once it is realized that the maintenance of capital is a human enterprise which may succeed or fail. It would be even more damaging, and not merely for the successful solution to some problems, but for the whole classical method of 'objectivist' plutology, if it were to become clear that this is a field in which different men confronting similar circumstances will take very different courses of action, while even courses similarly planned will sometimes succeed and sometimes fail. Devotees of classical plutology, past and present, have thus some reason to avert their eyes from this scene.

We now have to ask how problems concerning the maintenance of capital present themselves to the minds of capital owners and their agents, and how they may set about solving them. First of all, we have to distinguish between two groups of problems, problems germane to the making of 'right decisions', the planning of 'proper maintenance', and problems arising in the carrying out of such decisions, possibly in adverse circumstances. We shall use the word 'maintenance' here in the wider sense in which it includes repair and replacement of capital equipment.

The rationale of capital maintenance is the preservation in the future of an income stream presently flowing as regards both magnitude and desired time shape. The relevant decisions are therefore decisions about a time sequence of acts of maintenance (repair, replacement etc.) of individual capital goods which need not result in their physical preservation or replacement by replicas, but must result in the continued flowing of a desired income stream. They must, however, also include financial decisions about an expenditure stream adequate to defray costs of maintenance, to be set aside out of gross profits. Problems of the second kind mentioned above arise whenever gross profits turn out to be inadequate to support expenditure planned, so that these plans have to be revised.

A simple business rule of thumb, such as 'writing off all new plant and equipment within five years' has to be interpreted with regard to this framework of planning and decision-making if it is to make sense. In other words, we cannot hope to understand these forms of planning and action unless we make an attempt to understand how the problems they face present themselves to the minds of planners and plan administrators, and how they try to solve them. What amount exactly is to be written off? Neither original cost nor present market value will tell us that. Where the need for replacement arises at intervals, how are depreciation funds to be invested in the meantime? No such questions can be answered without allowing for planner's expectations.

In making decisions about maintenance of capital in a particular form at least three kinds of expectations (in reality far more) are typically involved:

1 expectations about the profitability of various output streams that might be produced with the help of the capital goods when maintained; it is to be noted that these involve the subjectivism of opportunity cost as well;
2 expectations about the availability and cost of resources complementary to the capital goods maintained, typically labour and energy ('giving hostages to future');
3 expectations about the adequacy of the gross profits required to ensure the future maintenance of capital goods to be maintained now. These expectations are not the same as under (1) since the most profitable part of an output stream may lie in the far future while the relevant part of the gross profits stream may be fairly near the present.

Any of these three (or other) kinds of expectations may turn out to be wrong; the outcome may be better or worse than expected by planners. If so, plans will have to be revised, in favourable circumstances perhaps in an 'upward' direction. This of course does not mean that capital cannot be maintained, but does mean that maintenance cannot take place *as originally planned*. A new problem presents itself.

Enough has been said to suggest that the maintenance of capital is always a problematic human activity.

IV

What conclusions are we to draw from the argument set forth? In the light of what has just been said, the statement that 'capital replaces itself' as a matter of course can now be seen to be highly misleading. In reality we are dealing here with a problem-solving activity which is sometimes successful and sometimes not. Our next task, then, must be to subject to critical review that whole body of economic thought for which successful maintenance of capital is a matter to be taken for granted. This clearly is a daunting task which, within the precinct of this chapter, can hardly be even adequately outlined, let alone attacked. All we can do here is to indicate the direction at least in which the critical effort of a catallactic theory of capital will have to tend.

The classical doctrine of the capital stock as 'an entity capable of maintaining its quantity while altering its form' (Pigou, 1935, p. 239) has to be the first candidate for our critical inspection.[5] As we have already dealt in chapter 1 with one aspect of this doctrine, the principle of the uniform rate of profits, and shown that in a world of unexpected change it is incapable of achievement, only a few remarks need be added here. Capital could be said to maintain its quantity while altering its form only if the maintenance of its value, while it is embodied in each of these forms, could be assured. But, as we have just seen, the maintenance of capital is always a problematic enterprise which may succeed or fail. There can be no such assurance.

A theory which takes the maintenance of capital for granted does not of course *ipso facto* lose all explanatory value. All human thought has to abstract from some facts. It all depends on how relevant the facts abstracted from are to the set of phenomena the theory claims to elucidate. This may not be a simple matter to ascertain where, for example, not the theory itself, but one of its corollaries is claimed to elucidate features of the real world.

The classical and neoclassical theories of distribution in which a 'surplus' or 'net product' is to be distributed between landlords, capitalists and workers, or between the 'factors of production', are for us a case in point. We have to take the maintenance of capital for granted in order to arrive at a determinate magnitude of the net distributable profit in each firm. We just saw that it cannot be taken for granted, and that the net profit of the firm depends in each case on expectations of its directors and accountants. Firms in the same industry, even if they all had the same physical assets, could earn the same rate of profit on them only if their directors put the same valuation on them and had them depreciated at the same rate. The concept of 'social surplus' or 'net product of society' as a macroeconomic magnitude is an even more bizarre notion, as it involves the aggregation of incommensurables, of figures based on different and, in the case of rival producers for example, often contradictory expectations.

Keynesian investment, the famous I = S, a fundamental concept of macroeconomics, is open to similar criticism. Keynes defined *current investment* as 'the current addition to the value of the capital equipment which has resulted from the productive activity of the period' (Keynes, 1936, p. 62). But if we cannot measure this capital equipment, but only evaluate it on the basis of divergent expectations, how do we know what constitutes an addition to it? Keynes saw the problem. 'But when Professor Hayek infers that the concepts of saving and investment suffer from a corresponding vagueness, he is only right if he means *net saving* and *net investment*. The *saving* and the *investment*, which are relevant to the theory of employment, are clear of this defect, and are capable of objective definition' (ibid. p. 60; italics in original). As, however, 'the *investment* of the period' is defined as the difference between A_1, 'the aggregate sales from one entrepreneur to another', and U_1 'the aggregate user costs of the entrepreneurs' (p. 62), and user cost, as we saw, is a subjective magnitude based on expectations, it is by no means clear why the Keynesian 'investment . . . relevant to the theory of employment' is 'clear of the defect' which, Keynes admitted, is inherent in the 'corresponding vagueness' surrounding the notion of net investment.

Quite apart from the problem of definition, there are practical issues here that cannot be ignored. It is of course well known that in practice, in the case of a concrete investment operation, it is often impossible to say how much is replacement and how much new investment. That investment opportunities exist primarily in the minds of investors is also recognized. The relationship between the success or failure of capital maintenance and the appearance or disappearance of investment opportunities appears to be less well understood.

An investment opportunity may owe its existence to an unexpected, but temporary, deterioration in the firm's position, in particular the loss of an indispensable item in the capital combination, or, in general, the failure of planned maintenance. Wherever gross profits are insufficient to support planned maintenance expenditure, new capital has to take the place of old capital lost. Successful maintenance, on the other hand, may render new investment superfluous, as when it is found that an old machine may be replaced by a new one that can also be used for other purposes. There is, however, also the possibility that successful maintenance may open up new opportunities for new investment in capital goods complementary to the existing ones.

Another corollary of the classical theory of distribution calling for review is the 'functionless capitalist'. The theory itself, to be sure, knows only profits which include the reward of the (innovating and opportunity-exploiting) entrepreneur as well as 'pure interest'. But once the division of capitalists into entrepreneurs and rentiers had been accepted, it seemed difficult to find a recognisable function for the latter. Now, however, we are able to say that it is impossible to receive a permanent income stream unless its source has been kept intact, and that this requires a problem-solving activity which may succeed or fail. Maintaining the value of capital resources is an important economic function.

Neoclassical theory, on the other hand, ascribes interest to the factor of production 'capital'. Here we encounter the difficulty with the 'entity capable of maintaining its quantity while altering its form' in a new guise. How are we to measure quantities of this factor? Owing to heterogeneity physical measurement is impossible, and even if it were possible would not help us since the return on capital must in any case be computed in value terms. Value measurement, on the other hand, is also impossible since capital values continuously fluctuate with expectations.

It seems to us much better to say that interest is an income which accrues to capital owners over and above the successful maintenance of their capital. It is not an income whose permanent flow can be taken for granted. It depends on the successful solution of a prior task. The fact that creditors and shareholders do not themselves have to solve this task but that their debtors, accountants and directors do it for them, though in the shareholders' case at their risk, seems irrelevant to the issue.

V

Success or failure of a firm's capital maintenance plan will of course affect other firms. Failure compelling maintenance plan revision will at first affect its immediate trading partners, but will later on have wider repercussions, as will any change in the firm's input, output or capital combination. As we watch the flow of goods move across an input-output table we have to remember that virtually all the transactions depicted here represent the maintenance of (mostly working) capital. We thus gain a clear view of the interaction of maintenance plans.

Structural complementarity, we said above, the complementarity of capital resources belonging to different firms trading with each other, gives rise to the problems of capital structure, the mode of composition of the capital stock of society.[6] The precarious nature of this complementarity stems from the fact that it has to rest on not just one plan, but on the congruence of several plans made to serve very different purposes. Thus, in the woollen textile industries, the equipment of the combing, spinning and weaving sections, as well as the stocks of cloth merchants, are structurally complementary, although each also forms part of the capital combination of the firm that owns it. Any plan revision in this whole sphere entailing a change in the flow of inputs and outputs will jeopardize the whole network of structural complementarity. The more plans are involved in this network, the more vulnerable is each type of equipment to plan revision by other owners. To make matters worse, the time horizons of the production plans of different firms will vary. The cloth merchants' plans need not involve a period longer than the longest period required for the turnover of their slowest-moving stock. Manufacturing firms need longer time horizons. It is quite possible that some time segments of the plans of different firms are compatible while others are not. This fact may evidently remain hidden for a time – until it is too late.

It is well known that in practice such problems are often overcome by long-term agreements between firms at adjacent stages of production involving coordination of long-term plans. In so far as other firms are excluded from such coordination of plans, such agreements are often regarded as 'monopolistic' in character. In reality they are part of the market process. In chapter 1 (p. 16) we saw that 'market processes consist of two phases succeeding each other in continuous iteration, which we may respectively describe as competition in the narrower sense and product variation'. These long-term marketing agreements between firms at adjacent stages have to be seen in a similar light.[7] While they of course, strictly speaking, restrict future competition, since the contracting parties cannot extend to others the favours they grant each other, such agreements are by no means 'in restraint of trade'. On the contrary, such trade as they engender could not come into existence without them. They constitute, in a sense, substitutes for futures markets which do not exist. The market process, as we saw, rests on divergent expectations, but, all the same, when there is clear need for convergent expectations, such as here, the market will devise a procedure to obtain it.

From what has been said in this chapter it seems to follow that capital phenomena are refractory to treatment in equilibrium terms. All such phenomena exist 'in time' while time is also the dimension of unexpected change. Moreover, it is hard to see how time can pass without concomitant change in the constellation of knowledge. In a world in which different men hold different expectations, some of these are bound to be disappointed and investment prompted by them will turn out as malinvestment. How, then, can there be equilibrium over time? At any moment the capital stock contains some 'fossils', capital goods which would not have come into existence, at least in their present forms, if the present situation had been correctly foreseen at the time of their investment. While it is true that they will gradually disappear, others will take their places. In a world of change it is hard to see how the capital stock of society can ever be said to have an 'equilibrium composition'.

The view set forth here is in striking contrast to another view of capital which, in the wake of the recent revival of the Ricardian style of thought, has been argued with remarkable verve. Its main exponent has been Professor Garegnani (1976, 1979), ably assisted by Dr Milgate (1979) and Professor Petri (1978). Their view is based on the classical concept of long-term equilibrium. 'As we all know, they understood the long-period position as the "centre" towards which the competitive economy would gravitate in the given long-period conditions. The basis of the argument had been laid down by Adam Smith with his distinction between the "market price" and "natural price" of a commodity' (Garegnani, 1976, p. 27). The stock of capital, defined as above by Pigou, is of course a 'datum' of this long-period position, and the 'normal rate of profits' one of its dependent variables.

It is clear that if we regard the capital stock as 'an entity capable of maintaining its quantity while altering its form', our 'fossils' do not really matter: they are but temporary forms of a permanent quantity. It is even possible to permit this quantity to change, and it does not even matter whether such change, accumulation or decumulation, is slow or rapid.

> That persistence was thought to ensure that changes in the causes, if continuous, would be sufficiently slow as not to endanger the gravitation towards the (slowly moving) long-period values. That same persistence would ensure that, should the changes be rapid, they would be once-for-all changes, and that, after a period of transition, gravitation to the new long-period values would again assert itself (ibid., p. 28).

But how, in any real situation, are we to distinguish between the effects of the paramount and the ephemeral forces? In particular, how are we to compute the 'normal rate of profits'? In Professor Joan Robinson's words 'Does he [Garegnani] mean what the rate of profit will be in the future or what it has been in the past, or does it float above historical time as a Platonic Idea?' (Robinson, 1979, p. 180).

In reply to this query Garegnani has now provided us with a clue to find our way from the puzzling world of market phenomena to the purer world of classical concepts. The normal rate of profits, he tells us,

> corresponds to the rate which is being realised *on an average* (as between firms and over time) by the entrepreneurs who use the dominant technique. This is so because these firms (like all other firms) will receive, on an average, the normal price for their product and pay, on an average, besides wages and rents, normal (supply) prices for the means of production to be replaced. But because this is the rate of profits which is being realised *in the present* under the stated conditions, it is also the rate of profits which that present experience will lead entrepreneurs to expect *in the future* from their current investment (Garegnani, 1979, p. 185; italics in original).

This passage offers us an almost perfect example on which to study the differences between the subjectivist and the 'objectivist', classical, approaches. We are all dealing with the same facts of a 'capitalistic' production economy, but these are seen here from a distorted perspective. The perspective is distorted because it has been devised by means of conceptual tools inadequate to the task of conveying to us the problems economic agents are struggling with in the real world.

In the first place, the last sentence of Garegnani's passage rests on a *non sequitur*: there is no reason why present profits, thought to be normal or otherwise, should last into the future. It is true that dealings in markets for securities often appear to be based on such a convention (dividend and earnings yields), but it is a convention more often honoured in the breach than in the observance.

Secondly, we have to note that firms' profits to be averaged are here tied to the 'dominant technique'. What happens when this changes and different firms qualify for inclusion in the average in different years? Moreover, who is to judge what is, at any moment, the dominant technique? In a world in which many firms are 'learning by doing' this is not obvious. No doubt, some of these techniques being learned now will turn out to be successful and others not, but this can only be known in the future, and not in that *present* the significance of which Garegnani wishes to stress.

Third, the second sentence referring to 'normal (supply) prices for the means of production to be replaced' ignores most of the problems of capital maintenance discussed above. It makes sense only in a world in which we already know how to replace old capital goods. Moreover, what is present profit depends no less on expectations of future revenue than on present magnitudes. If capital maintenance plans fail and losses are suffered, the quantity of our 'entity' itself is diminished and our 'centre of gravity' impaired.

Finally, it is hard to see what light an inter-firm average might cast on the conduct of individual firms. Rival producers may not even know one another's profits and would have to show a touching faith in balance-sheet figures were they to act as Garegnani wants them to. Each firm knows that profit figures depend on expectations reflected in depreciation amounts, and can hardly be unaware that such expectations differ among firms. To base one's investment plans on an average of figures known to be inspired by the divergent expectations of one's rivals seems to be an odd way of going about one's business.

VI

In this chapter we have made an attempt to contribute to an endeavour to lay the foundations of a catallactic theory of capital, and to make us see the problems of capital formation and use from the perspective of individuals acting rather than that of detached observers. Inevitably, a good deal of this chapter has taken the form of a critique of classical plutology.

Sir John Hicks, however, though the author of the dichotomy plutology–catallactics, has twice told us that in the history of thought on capital another dichotomy is of great importance, that of 'fundism' versus 'materialism' (Hicks, 1963, pp. 342–8, and 1974, pp. 307–16):

> I am going to maintain that the distinction is quite ancient; it divides economists, ancient and modern, into two camps. There are some for whom Real Capital is a Fund I shall call them Fundists, and there are some for whom it consists of physical goods . . . I shall venture in this paper to call them Materialists (Hicks, 1974, p. 309).

It soon becomes evident that, despite appearances, the two Hicksian dichotomies do not coincide.

Not only Adam Smith, but all (or nearly all) of the British Classical Economists were Fundists, so was Marx . . ., so was Jevons. It was after 1870 that there was a Materialist Revolution. It is not the same as the Marginalist Revolution; for some of the Marginalists, such as Jevons and Böhm-Bawerk, kept the Fundist flag flying. But most economists, in England and in America, went Materialist. Materialism, indeed, is characteristic of what is nowadays reckoned to be the, neoclassical position (ibid.).

In the middle of this century, however, there came a change in the wake of the Keynesian revolution. 'But the rethinking of capital theory and of growth theory, which followed from Keynes, and from Harrod on Keynes, led to a revival of Fundism. If the Production Function is a hallmark of Materialism, the capital–output ratio is a hallmark of modern Fundism' (ibid.). Later on we are told that 'Hayek, of course, was a Fundist, but a very sophisticated Fundist, deeply preoccupied with the problems of ignorance and uncertainty which came to the fore as soon as one thinks of capital value as being determined by expectations of the future (ibid., p. 315).

Much of this was bound to sound odd to those who remembered the fierce controversy of the 1930s on Austrian capital theory[8] and, in particular, Professor Hayek's attack on Knight in 1936.

This basic mistake – if the substitution of a meaningless statement for the solution of a problem can be called a mistake – is the idea of capital as a fund which maintains itself automatically, and that, in consequence, once an amount of capital has been brought into existence the necessity of reproducing it presents no economic problem (Hayek, 1936, p. 357).

In the course of this argument Hayek saw himself compelled to disavow Böhm-Bawerk: 'The Böhm-Bawerkian theory in particular went astray in assuming, with the older views that Professor Knight now wants to revive, that the quantity of capital (or the "possibility to wait") was a simple magnitude, a homogeneous fund of clearly determinate size' (ibid., p. 374).[9]

It is even odder that Böhm-Bawerk in 1907 explicitly rejected Clark's notion of capital as 'a permanent abiding fund of productive wealth'. How are we to reconcile this fact with Hicks's description of Clark as 'clearly materialist' while Böhm-Bawerk, we saw, 'kept the Fundist flag flying'?

What are we to make of all this? It is clear that Hicksian Fundism is not the same thing as the Knightian Fundism Hayek denounced. But what, if any, is the relationship between them?

We shall learn that, up to a point, the second Hicksian dichotomy serves to elucidate problems of planning and action concerning capital, while, even when that point has been reached, it may still be of use to us in enabling us to catch an occasional glimpse of some of the happenings in the realm of shadows that lies beyond its cone of light.

In trying to clarify these intriguing problems we do not get much help from arguments designed to show that capital is, and can be, 'nothing but' the totality of material resources at our disposal, and that talking of a fund constitutes an illegitimate duplication of this totality. Let us look at the facts.

In the first place, capital goods have to exist in the minds of agents no less than in reality. In fact, their significance for action derives from the places they occupy in individual plans, that is, from the mental acts by which plans are constituted. Such significance may change, without any change in 'material circumstances', merely as a result of changing expectations, of changing thoughts. If so, we need a language in which to express such changing significance of unchanging material resources. To call this 'mythology' would be to cut at the roots of subjectivism.

In other words, capital goods have a value dimension as well as their physical dimensions. While in terms of the latter capital is of course heterogeneous, in terms of the former diverse capital goods may be reduced to homogeneity. In fact, in planning and carrying out plans this has to be done since the planner has to match means with ends and, except for sums of money, almost all his means are capital goods. He has to evaluate them in order to make them commensurable to each other as well as to his ends. Every plan, simply for the sake of the comparability of the means it employs, has to assign values to its capital inputs. Plan failure and consequent revision will probably entail changes in the evaluation of capital goods, but it is a peculiar aspect of our problem that, even while a plan proceeds satisfactorily with no unexpected change in workshop or market, planners may have reason to change capital values. Changes in the value dimension may not be accompanied by any other 'observable' event.

It is natural for business men to regard their stock of means as a revolving fund. This metaphor simply lends expression to the fact that inputs have to be made, and outputs accrue, continuously. Everybody knows that unexpected change may interfere with the constant revolving motion, that capital gains and losses may occur. From time to time accountants and business men have to revalue capital goods and thus the magnitude of their fund. If we were to find a macro-economic equivalent of such corrective action, we should be well on our way towards a coordination of micro- and macro-economics.

On the surface, Hicksian Fundism has an enchanting attraction since in the notion of the fund it appears to provide us with a basis for the social aggregation of capital combinations privately held and directed, for the macro-integration of micro-entities. It seems to enable us to regard the capital stock of society as the sum total of all those revolving funds that keep millions of businesses going, itself something of a super-fund. This of course is the way Ricardo looked at the capital stock.

Alas, in reality it cannot be done. The notion of the capital stock as a revolving super-fund requires of course the coordination of all capital maintenance plans, as we should find it in a stationary state or an economy in 'steady growth'. Outside them, as we saw, such coordination cannot exist. Sooner or later, the mechanism of the super-fund is bound to become clogged as some of the cog-wheels in our clockwork begin to turn at different speeds.

In this chapter we have now seen that the Realm of Capital is a particularly fertile source of unexpected change continuously engendered by incoherent capital maintenance plans. The reflection of these changes in asset markets in the form of capital gains and losses is of course well known. In the markets for capital goods and titles to them intersubjective differences of perspective and intertemporal changes in them are of paramount importance. The significance of the former is attested by the permanent existence of bulls and bears in the Stock Exchanges and great commodity markets of the world, that of the latter by the ebb and flow of capital gains and losses.

At a first glance it may appear that these asset market phenomena, engendered by changing expectations and hence by 'speculative' activity, must be regarded as *exogenous* to the sphere of production. In this chapter we have endeavoured to show, however, that and why in the sphere of capital such a distinction is as futile as it was in the case of technical progress.

From time to time, all capital goods have to be revalued, and such revaluation is bound to have far-reaching consequences. It matters very little whether the immediate cause of such revaluation is the actual failure of plans for the production and maintenance of capital goods or a 'mere change in thoughts' about the future. In all cases it is the change in perspective of some agent that matters.

NOTES

1 For some consequences of this fact for Austrian capital theory, see Lachmann (1978), pp. viii–ix.
2 For classical theory, by contrast, 'in a long-period equilibrium, the composition of the capital endowment (i.e. the proportions between the endowments of the various capital goods) is not given in advance, but is rather part of the problem of the determination of the equilibrium, while, conversely, if the composition of capital is a datum, then a long-period equilibrium cannot be determined. The implication is that disaggregation does not overcome the need to measure the capital endowment as an amount of value, as long as one tries to determine a long-period equilibrium' (Petri, 1978, p. 247).
3 'Once capital is definitely and irrevocably committed to a certain purpose, any of the cooperating factors are capable, through monopolistic combination, of forcing the capitalists to pass on to them part of the gross returns which ought to be re-invested but which, if paid out as income to non-capitalists, will be mostly consumed' (Hayek, 1941, p. 346).
4 For an intriguing discussion on the role of the postulate of the 'reproducibility of the system' in the 'classical Marxian' tradition, see Hollis and Nell (1975), chapter 9, esp. pp. 245–50.
5 In Professor Petri's formulation, 'it was so important to have a concept of capital as a single homogeneous quantity which can take various shapes, like a fluid which could change its shape from one to another kind of capital goods. This left the composition of capital free to adapt itself to the requirements of a long-period equilibrium. The type of equilibrium that this approach tried to determine included an equilibrium composition of capital' (Petri, 1978, p. 257).
   We may note that though 43 years (and the Ricardian revival!) lie between the two formulations, the interpretation of the capital requirements of classical long-period equilibrium has not changed.
6 See Lachmann (1978), chapters IV and V.
7 This was first emphasized by G. B. Richardson (1960).
8 See Kirzner (1976), pp. 133–43, also Kirzner (1966), pp. 61–70.
9 Once we remember that Böhm-Bawerk was as much a Ricardian as an Austrian, we shall not find it at all strange that Milgate, as a neo-Ricardian critic of neoclassical decadence, feels bound to defend him against Hayek's strictures. 'What distinguishes Hayek's view of the purpose that

the notion of intertemporal equilibrium was to serve from that of his contemporaries is that he was, at times, prepared to admit the fundamental break with tradition that it involved' (Milgate, 1979, p. 8). In other words, Böhm-Bawerk did not 'go astray', but upheld the common classical tradition.

5

Money and the Market Process

'Monetary theory is less abstract than most economic theory; it cannot avoid a relation to reality, which in other economic theory is sometimes missing. It belongs to monetary history, in a way that economic theory does not always belong to economic history' (Hicks, 1967, p. 156).

This simple truth has a number of implications. We encounter some of them when we begin to ask what a rôle money plays in the market process. In a general equilibrium model money may either be an exogenous or an endogenous force, it cannot be both at the same time. But the Market Process is a historical process unfolding in real time. There is no reason why, at different periods of history, money might not at some times impinge on market events from outside while at other times forming an integral part of these events. A timeless theory of money is hardly feasible.

Within the last hundred years the Western world has witnessed the transition from metallic money to bank money, from the Gold Standard to a pure credit economy in which bank liabilities are the commonly accepted means of payment. During the last three decades this process was accompanied, in modern industrial countries, by the rapid rise of a sophisticated financial system based on intermediation. It would be odd indeed if any theory of money had survived unscathed a process of transformation of such dimensions. What we find in fact is that monetary theorists, addicted to high levels of abstraction and averse to taking cognizance of historical change, during the period repeatedly saw themselves compelled to 're-state' their theories.

The quantity theory is an obvious case in point. As long as gold and silver were money, the quantity of money was an entirely unproblematical notion. The same applies to an issue of paper money, for example as the monetized part of the government debt. When credit instruments become money, on the other hand, quantitative precision is lost. In a credit economy the definition of money becomes notoriously difficult. However we define it, it is usually surrounded by a penumbra of close money-substitutes which may be accepted as money in some parts of the market, but possibly not in others. So even the rule 'Money is what the market accepts as money' often becomes hard to apply. But the greatest obstacle to the applicability of the quantity theory to a credit economy lies in the simple fact that credit is created and destroyed by acts of human minds while the quantity of gold or silver existing at any time is not subject to such vagaries.

It is true that banks are almost everywhere subject to certain rules which set limits to their activity, but it is also true that within these bounds an area of freedom remains. Sir John Hicks described the situation in these terms:

> There is no question . . . that when money is a metallic money, its supply can be treated as an exogenous variable; major changes in supply, at least, come in from 'outside'. But the supply of bank money is not clearly exogenous. It can indeed be affected by changes in banking policy, but with given policy (as represented, more or less, by given lending rates) the supply of bank money is determined by the market. It is provided by the banks, to the extent that the market requires, so it is *not* an exogenous variable. It is true that this may be in practice concealed (or partly concealed) in so far as the banking system works under rules, that have been imposed upon it, rules which maintain some form of attachment between the supply of bank money and an external base (in the Gold Standard period the supply of gold). If the rules were completely firm, the supply of bank money would then be a function of the supply of gold, and of that only – so that the supply of bank money, also, could be regarded as an exogenous variable. That is what a Quantity theory, in those new conditions, must imply (Hicks 1977, pp. 59–60).

It would be better not to say that under a Gold Standard demand for money adjusts itself to the supply while in a credit economy the supply of credit adjusts itself to the demand for it. Tendencies in these directions doubtless exist. The reason for caution is that the first statement, while true, fails to tell us how it happens, while the second is by no means always true. In most normal circumstances a fringe of unsatisfied borrowers will continue to exist. It is better to say that in a credit economy supply is more elastic, if more complex, than in one tied to a metallic standard, that life in a credit economy poses more problems, some soluble as well as some insurmountable, and offers economic agents more opportunities at the same time as confronting them with more paths of peril.

It has to be remembered that even under the Gold Standard, as it existed in the Western world between 1879 and 1914, a credit pyramid gradually grew up on the metallic basis. Even a relatively simple industrial economy of, say, the mid-Victorian type could not of course exist without credit. Most of the phenomena we are about to examine did, then, exist, if *in nuce*, during that period. When did the modern credit economy come into existence? We might perhaps say that the transition had taken place when the majority of business men came to regard their bank deposits as 'cash', and no longer as credit granted to the bank. Like all attempts to mark the boundaries of periods of history, however, this one has to be used with some caution.

II

There are several reasons why the modern credit economy does not readily lend itself to an interpretation in terms of the quantity theory. We have already mentioned the difficulty of having to indicate which credit instruments are money and which are not, and the embarrassing plenitude of money substitutes. But the main impediment is to be found in the mechanistic style of thought which has engendered the quantity theory, while the phenomena of a credit economy call for a subjectivist approach and lend themselves to an interpretative style of thought.

The granting of credit requires the consent of at least two persons, a creditor and a debtor. For its continued existence the credit relationship requires the continued consent of both, while the continued existence of a gold coin does not depend on such conditions. The creation of a credit relationship requires a meeting of at least two minds, while an act of will on the part of one suffices to destroy it. Hence uncertainty of each partner about the continued willingness of the other to maintain the credit relationship is of the essence of this relationship. Credit may of course be granted for a minimum period, or a fixed period altogether, but uncertainty about what will happen after it has expired remains. This convergence of purposes necessary to maintain a given credit relationship, and uncertainty about its continued existence, impart to the monetary system of a credit economy an instability inherent in these circumstances and absent from that of a metallic standard. A given 'volume of credit' may persist for a long time, but if so, it owes its persistence to a remarkable coincidence of the purposes pursued by creditors and debtors, while the persistence of a given quantity of gold or silver in a given space calls for no such explanatory efforts on our part.

The next feature of credit money we have to take into account is the costlessness of its creation while metal has to be mined and coins have to be struck.

> That is the reason why the credit system grows: that it provides a medium of exchange at much lower cost. But on the other side there is the penalty that the credit system is an unstable system. It rests upon confidence and trust; when trust is absent it can just shrivel up. It is unstable in the other direction too; when there is too much confidence or optimism it can explode in bursts of speculation. Thus in order for a credit system to work smoothly, it needs an institutional framework which shall restrain it on the one hand, and shall support it on the other (Hicks, 1967, p. 158).

In a credit economy a particular kind of costly knowledge is continuously required and has to be safeguarded against obsolescence. Creditors must have some knowledge about the circumstances of their debtors while debtors must have some knowledge about alternative sources of credit should the one presently used fail. In a rapidly changing world all such knowledge has to be monitored. This is not the general learnable knowledge of science and technology which, emanating from one central source, may be disseminated to many. The knowledge here required is very 'decentralized', and is specific knowledge of particular circumstances. Every debtor has a different set of prospects and a different asset portfolio. In Professor Hahn's words, 'The possibility of bankruptcy is alone sufficient to make of every demand for a loan a "named" demand. That is, every debt differs by the actual borrower' (Hahn, 1977, p. 37). We also have to note that the uncertainty here involved is a multiple uncertainty, about what is the case today and about what may happen next week. Gold mines, by contrast, do not have to worry about debtors.

From this uncertainty stems the need for reserve assets held against debts as a characteristic trait of the credit economy, and the multiplication of this need as the financial system grows in complexity by the multiplication of stages of intermediation.

> It is this, more than anything else, which makes the Quantity theory inapplicable to the pure credit economy. The Quantity of Money must now mean the Quantity of bank money; but a substantial part of the Quantity of bank money is now, in principle, idle. So the total Quantity of Money may vary considerably, while the part which is not idle is substantially unchanged. The link between the total Quantity of Money and that part of it which circulates is effectively snapped. (Hicks, 1977, p. 63).

In any monetary system, of course, producers and merchants have to hold cash reserves against their liabilities and other contingencies. What is specific to the modern financial system based on credit intermediation is the need for *additional* reserve assets to be held against debt money. The more stages of debt creation there are, for the same volume of credit, the more reserve assets are required.

In a credit economy some credits are opened every day while others are closed. The latter may have been called in by creditors, or have expired as originally stipulated, or have been repaid prematurely by debtors finding themselves more liquid than they had anticipated. It takes two to create credit, as we saw, but only one to wipe it out.

In a money economy goods and services are not exchanged for goods and services but for money. Say's Law does not operate unless money is metallic and we regard the metal as a good. It is true that the creation and cancellation of credit in a credit economy can have no effects that might not be produced by dishoarding or hoarding of metallic money, but we have to remember that the volume of such dishoarding is limited by the existing hoards and these by the quantity of money. On the other hand, while no credit can be repaid that was not earlier brought into existence, there is, in principle, no limit to credit creation.

Hoarding and dishoarding affect relative prices, if these are flexible, where their impact falls unevenly on different parts of the economic system. So do credit expansion and contraction. In fixprice markets both phenomena cause unplanned growth or decline of stocks.

Having elucidated these circumstances we now are able to turn to the question what part money plays in the market process. We saw that hoarding and dishoarding, credit creation and contraction, are, all four, disequilibrating activities. By the same token, they must play a part in the market process. As we saw, credit creation and contraction can produce no phenomena that hoarding and dishoarding would not produce under a metallic standard. But the quantitative dimensions the four activities might assume are of course entirely different. Under a gold standard there is some, but restricted, scope for hoarding. In a credit economy the scope for credit creation is virtually unlimited.

To designate, in these circumstances, a relatively small number of credit instruments as 'high-powered money', and to try to relate quantitative change in them to a number of macroeconomic aggregates does not strike one as a promising venture in monetary theory.

The market process, as we learnt earlier, is impelled by exogenous forces impinging on the economic system and the sequence of constellations of divergent expectations. As regards the former, the credit pattern, continuously shifting for the reasons discussed, may in our case well be said to play the part of such an exogenous force.

As regards expectations, however, the part they play in the modern credit economy is rather more difficult to characterize as they are bound to appear in the form of exogenous as well as endogenous forces. Credit, in the sense of the transfer of wealth to those who can make better use of it than its owners, is probably as old as the market economy and long preceded the modern credit system. Of course it always has to rest on appropriate expectations.

Many of the expectations which in the modern credit economy prompt producers, merchants and asset holders to seek and obtain credit would before its time at best have remained figments of the imagination. In our world they can become exogenous forces impinging upon the economic system by virtue of the fact that the latter has engendered the endogenous forces which shape the credit pattern. On the other hand of course, the operation of the modern credit economy gives rise to inflationary and deflationary expectations of its own which affect relative prices and manifest themselves *inter alia* in the taking up of bull and bear positions which collapse if credit is withdrawn from their holders. As is typical of social processes, the sequence of constellations of divergent expectations which serves to lend shape to the market process is the complex result of the interplay of creative acts of the minds of market participants with forces exogenous and endogenous to the economic system.

In what follows we shall examine various stages of the evolution of monetary thought in this century. In doing so we shall have to bear in mind the question to what extent they reflect the facts just discussed.

III

It seems to us that, when we cast a glance at the development of the theory of money over the past 70 years, there is discernible a broad tendency we might describe as a *thrust towards subjectivism*. By this we mean a skein of thought within which at least three strands are distinguishable. We see, in the first place, a tendency to substitute explanations couched in terms of means and ends, of purposes sought, for mechanistic explanations; in the second place, an emphasis on action rather than reaction, on active minds finding their orientation in a daily changing world rather than on human 'dispositions'. Action, guided by plans, involves a period of time, a future as well as a present, while in reaction, where there can be no time interval between it and that which is being reacted to (lest the latter slip away while we are taking thought), everything happens at one windowless moment. The third strand is a readiness to accept the fact that a timeless world is not conceivable, that we are for ever moving from an irrevocable past into an unknowable future. In facing this future men have to act on their expectations which differ between men. Hence expectations are typically divergent, and the subjectivism of expectations has to complement the subjectivism of preferences.

It is of course impossible to indicate any particular period in the history of economic thought as the date of birth of our thrust towards subjectivism, just as it is impossible to indicate a date of birth for subjectivist thought in economics in general. While therefore any choice of a date as the starting-point of the period of our study is necessarily arbitrary, there may be some virtue in choosing a point of time at which the main opposite tendency was still strong and visible, brightly gleaming in the sun of success, and at which its characteristic features had not yet become blurred by the need, on the part of its exponents, to hide some of the traits of its decline.

We therefore choose 1911, the year of publication of Irving Fisher's *Purchasing Power of Money*. There can be no doubt at all that this was a most successful book. No author could wish for more. By setting the old classical quantity theory, an empirical generalization about the causal relationship between the quantity of money and the price level, against the framework of the famous equation $MV = PT$, that is, a truism, the author succeeded in showing under what conditions it would hold. The mere fact that after 1911 most of the critics of the quantity theory found it necessary to turn their fire on this equation in itself attests the success of Fisher's book.

Seen from a different historical perspective, however, the story looks rather different. The quantity theory, we might say, which had played an indispensable part in the classical system, had by 1911 lost it and not as yet acquired a new one. As is well known, to classical economists the value of money was a source of embarrassment and confusion. It did not appear to fit into classical plutology: unlike land and capital resources money was not a source of wealth but was regarded as 'barren'. Nor did it fit into the scheme of the classical cost-of-production theory of value. While it was tempting enough to explain the value of metallic money by mining costs, too many cases of paper money that had value were known to be overlooked. In the end money came to be regarded as simply a 'veil' behind which, and unencumbered by which, all real economic processes of production and distribution take place.

In this classical scheme of thought the quantity theory had an obvious part to play. While relative values were determined by real economic forces behind the veil, the quantity of money then served to convert them into money values. The 'classical dichotomy' thus came to rest on the quantity theory.

But the demise of classical plutology and the rise of utility theories of value in the 1870s brought a change of scene also here. Marget put it clearly:

> It is, indeed, hardly an accident that writers, such as Walras and Menger, who in their writings on the general theory of value, were insistent upon referring the phenomena of the market back to the choices of 'economizing' individuals, should, in their writings on money, have also been protagonists of the cash-balance approach . . . . The important point for our present purpose . . . is the corollary to be drawn from the general methodological principle when it is applied to the special case in hand. This corollary is simply that if, instead of being content merely to record the fact that 'velocity' is at a given level, we wish – in the words of Marshall – to unravel the *causes that govern* the rapidity of circulation of the currency', we must, as always whenever we attempt to explain how market values are determined, put ourselves in the position of the individuals engaged in market processes, and ask what they do which is relevant to the particular market process in which we are interested, and why they do it (Marget, 1938, pp. 418–19).[1]

In this passage we have a lucid, if not a succinct, statement of what we may call '*monetary subjectivism*'. Marget rightly also stresses the role of Menger and Walras as protagonists of the 'cash-balance approach' in the theory of money. Indeed, in 1912, the year following the publication of Fisher's book, Mises stated the main tenets of this approach, and hence of monetary subjectivism, with admirable precision and elegance in his *Theorie des Geldes und der Umlaufsmittel*.

The fact remains that at the time, partly no doubt owing to the fact that Fisher's book was published in English, while Mises's was in German, the attention of economists in the Anglo-Saxon world was centred on the Fisher equation, and the quantity theory had a revival. As a result the next step in the progress of monetary subjectivism took the form of the introduction of what has come to be known as the *Cambridge k* into the quantity equation. In 1917 Pigou presented the equation

$$P = \frac{kR}{M}$$

where R is the 'total resources, expressed in terms of wheat, that are enjoyed by the community; k the proportion of these resources that it chooses to keep in the form of titles to legal tender; M the number of units of legal tender; and P the value, or price, per unit of these titles, in terms of wheat' (Pigou, 1917, p. 42).

If 'resources' here means output, and not wealth, Pigou's equation represents as much of a truism as does Fisher's Quantity Equation. What matters to us is that the introduction of k connotes the infusion of a dose of subjectivism into a set of relationships which did not seem to offer much scope for acts of human minds. We also may note that, while the T of the Fisher equation refers to all transactions for which money may be used, the R of the Pigou equation, at least in the interpretation we give it, refers to output currently sold. It is of course possible to give the Fisher equation a narrower interpretation and to substitute in it R for T. In this case its V becomes the expression for income velocity rather than transactions velocity, and therefore the inverse of k. Our next task will be to examine Keynes's criticism of the 'Cambridge' quantity equation in his *Treatise on Money*. Since in our view Keynes's work, in the *Treatise* and later on, made notable contributions to the progress of monetary subjectivism, his criticism of an earlier stage of it calls for our attention.

Keynes wrote:

The element of confusion is this. If we are to interest ourselves in the relationship between the average stock of money and the national income, we must mean by the former the average stock held by the members of the public as enjoyers of income, i.e. the income-deposits, and not the total stock of money including the business-deposits. The relationship between the total annual receipts of income-receivers and the average stock of money held by them is one thing, which we call the velocity of the income-deposits; and the relationship between the total flow of transactions for all purposes and the average stock of money held for all purposes is another thing, which we call the velocity of the cash-deposits. But the relationship between the total annual receipts of income-receivers and the average stock of money held for all purposes is a hybrid conception having no particular significance. Yet it is something of this kind which turns up in economic literature over and over again. . . . It is as though we were to divide the passenger-miles travelled in an hour by passengers in trains by the aggregate number of passengers in trams and trains and to call the result a 'velocity' (Keynes, 1930, vol. II, pp. 24–5).

Keynes, we note, here insists on the division of the total stock of money into various parts each serving a different purpose. He does not demand that we provide a micro-foundation for a macro-aggregate. He wants us to divide a large macro-aggregate into a number of smaller such aggregates. Nevertheless, as the purposes of a certain kind of human action are to serve us as the criteria of the division proposed, we have to regard the proposal as a step along the path of monetary subjectivism.

In his *Treatise* Keynes pleaded for the Quantity Equation to be replaced by his own 'Fundamental Equations for the Value of Money' to be found in chapter 10. As he abandoned them very soon in favour of other conceptual tools, little need to be said about them at this date. The substitute recommended for the 'hybrid conception' of income velocity, however, is a matter of considerable interest to us. In the famous chapter 15, in the spirit of his critical remarks on income velocity quoted above, he divided the total stock of money into the industrial and the financial circulation:

By *Industry* we mean the business of maintaining the normal process of current output, distribution and exchange and paying the factors of production their incomes for the various duties which they perform . . . .

> By *Finance*, on the other hand, we mean the business of holding and exchanging existing titles to wealth (other than exchanges resulting from the specialisation of industry), including Stock Exchange and Money Market transactions, speculation and the process of conveying current savings and profits into the hands of entrepreneurs. Each of these two branches of Business utilises a certain part of the total stock of money (vol. I, p. 243).

This statement calls for two observations. In the first place, the two spheres mentioned can maintain their separate existence only for very short periods. If bank clerks are paid monthly, money flows from the financial into the industrial circulation once monthly and of course other money flows in the opposite direction. But, secondly, the words 'financial circulation' are in fact a misnomer. What Keynes really means are money balances *held*, not money flowing from buyers to sellers. He readily admits 'as a result of the great development of devices for economizing the use of cash by Stock Exchange clearings and the like – that the *absolute* amount of the variations in the volume of money so employed cannot ordinarily be very great' (vol. I, p. 249).

But, quite apart from our two observations, what really matters is that transactions in the two spheres serve entirely different purposes.

> But the volume of trading in financial instruments, i.e. the *activity* of financial business, is not only highly variable but has no close connection with the volume of output whether of capital-goods or of consumption-goods; for the current output of fixed capital is small compared with the existing stock of wealth, which in the present context we will call the volume of *securities* (excluding from this liquid claims on cash); and the activity with which these securities are being passed round from hand to hand does not depend on the rate at which they are being added to. Thus in a modern Stock-Exchange-equipped community the turnover of currently produced fixed capital is quite a small proportion of the total turnover of securities. (Vol. I, pp. 248–9).

Hence, interest rates cannot serve to bring planned investment and planned savings to equality. Their real economic function is to enable the many markets which serve the exchange of existing stocks of wealth to clear, for instance the bond market. Since activity on such markets is governed by the divergence of expectations, the 'bullishness' and 'bearishness' of the public, the passage quoted, and the chapter 15 from which it is taken, mark, in a most significant sense, the introduction of expectations into Anglo-Saxon economics, at least into its market theory, its catallactics.[2]

In the financial circulation, expectations are of importance not merely because the range of their divergence governs the volume of exchange transactions, but also for another reason: the stock of money held in the financial sphere to a large extent reflects the 'bear position'. This term, we are told, is

> including, however, as bears not only those who have sold securities 'short', i.e. have sold securities which they do not own, but also those who would normally be holders of securities but prefer for the time being to hold liquid claims on cash in the form of Savings-deposits. A 'bear', that is to say, is one who prefers at the moment to avoid securities and lend cash, and correspondingly a 'bull' is one who prefers to hold securities and borrow cash – the former anticipating that securities will fall in cash value and the latter that they will rise (Keynes, 1930, vol. I, p. 250).

IV

Before we set out on our way to follow the thrust towards subjectivism in Keynes's work from the *Treatise* to the *General Theory*, we have to turn aside briefly to consider an episode of the 1930s which is of some significance to our theme, namely Professor Hicks's 'Suggestion for Simplifying the Theory of Money', a paper originally read at the London Economic Club in November 1934 (Hicks, 1967, pp. 61–82). If we may say that in Keynes's *Treatise* monetary subjectivism as a major theme is implicit rather than explicit, there can be little doubt that in Hicks's paper it found articulate expression.

Professor Hicks starts by describing the surprise felt by somebody like himself who, brought up in the theory of value, came over to monetary theory and discovered that a familiar landmark was missing there: 'It was marginal utility that really made sense of the theory of value; and to come to a branch of economics which does without marginal utility altogether! No wonder there are such difficulties and such differences! What is wanted is a "marginal revolution"!' (p. 62). Perhaps it might have been better to speak here of the need for a subjective rather than a 'marginal' revolution.

Hicks makes his main point early on: 'The essence of the method I am proposing is that we should take the position of an individual at a particular point of time, and inquire what determines the precise quantity of money which he will desire to hold' (p. 64). Why is it important to conduct our inquiry "at a particular point of time"? The answer is significant:

> A very large amount of current controversy about money seems to me to be due to the attempt, superficially natural, but, in fact, highly inconvenient, to establish a close relation between the demand for money and *income*. Now the simple consideration that the decision to hold money is always made at a point of time shows that the connexion between income and the demand for money must always be indirect (pp. 64–5).

In other words, when we wish to apply utility analysis to the demand for money and ask why money is held, we must realize that this question can meaningfully be asked only with respect to a point of time, not a period of time. We are asking for the reasons for a decision, and, although action, to be sure, always takes time, the decision to act can only be taken at a point of time. It may or may not be adhered to in subsequent periods of time, but, whatever happens later on, a decision, an act of our mind, belongs to a point of time and involves orientation to the state of knowledge present at it. According to a well-know Austrian axiom, 'Time cannot elapse without the state of knowledge changing.' Decisions to act, by contrast, require a (temporarily) fixed state of knowledge to permit us to find our orientation in the position we happen to be in. As Shackle was to put it many years later 'Situation is stock, transformation is flow' (Shackle, 1972, p. 413).

As regards money, the corollary of the praxeological insight we have just gained is that the function of money involved in the inquiry into the causes of the demand for money is its store-of-value function, and not its medium-of-exchange function. For while the latter requires a period of time in order to be exercised by repeated exchange against a flow of goods and services, the exercise of the former pertains to a part of an individual's stock of wealth as it exists at a moment in time. Here the significance of the fact that, while there is no substitute for money as a medium of exchange, there are indeed many substitutes for it as an item of wealth, is reflected in the circumstance that we demand an explanation why any wealth is held in the form of money, and any such explanation of course has to run in terms of the situation as perceived by the owner or manager of the stock of wealth at a point of time, including his expectations about events in subsequent periods. No approach to money which ignores the point-of-time character of the various forms in which wealth may be deployed holds out much promise to get to the bottom of monetary problems. The mutability of expectations as time passes is of course only an outward symptom of this state of affairs. What we called the 'second strand' of monetary subjectivism is intimately involved in all these problems.

Hicks expresses this by demanding a framework for the rôle of money as an item of wealth in the form 'not of an income account, but of a capital account, a balance-sheet. We have to concentrate on the forces which make assets and liabilities what they are.' He explains his demand by telling us that 'my suggestion can be expressed by saying that we ought to regard every individual in the community as being, on a small scale, a bank. Monetary theory becomes a sort of generalization of banking theory' (Hicks, 1967, p. 74).

The drawing-up of a balance sheet involves the evaluation of assets. There thus emerges the problem of the subjectivism of expectations as involved in this activity. It is noteworthy how reluctantly (in 1934!) our author came to embrace monetary subjectivism, and how stubbornly he would cling to an 'objectivism' denied by the very trend of his whole approach.

> If I am right, the whole problem of applying monetary theory is largely one of deducing changes in anticipations from the changes in objective data which call them forth. Obviously, this is not an easy task, and above all, it is not one which can be performed in a mechanical fashion. It needs judgement and knowledge of business psychology much more than sustained logical reasoning. The armchair economist will be bad at it, but he can at least begin to realize the necessity for it, and learn to co-operate with those who can do it better than he can (p. 76).

If 'objective data' no longer lend themselves to deductions made from them 'in a mechanical fashion', but require such subjective elements as 'judgement', involving presumably differences in perspective, do they, then, not lose their 'objective' character by virtue of the fact that they are no longer the same to everybody?

Hicks's main conclusion, however, was in the spirit of subjectivism: that it is hard to link the demand for money to any other economic force without having at once to face exceptions to the rule. It may be tempting to say that the demand for money is a decreasing function of wealth, but may there not be people who have lost wealth recently and now need more money than they would in proportion to any such function? So we had better tread warily. 'There is no reason why policies which tend to economic welfare, statically considered, should also tend to monetary stability. Indeed, the presumption is rather the other way round' (p. 82).

In turning to examine the impact of the thrust towards subjectivism on Keynes' *General Theory*, as compared with his *Treatise*, we find, at least on the surface, little that is new or exciting except nomenclature. To be sure, the industrial and financial circulations are now called *active* and *idle money* respectively; saving and investment, being equal by definition, can no longer affect price levels by their difference, and Keynes now distinguishes clearly between the price level of capital goods and the marginal efficiency of capital, an expectational magnitude. The demand for money, now called *liquidity-preference*,

> may be defined as depending on (I) the transactions-motive, i.e. the need of cash for the current transaction of personal and business exchanges; (II) the precautionary-motive, i.e. the desire for security as to the future cash equivalent of a certain proportion of total resources; and (III) the speculative-motive, i.e. the object of securing profit from knowing better than the market what the future will bring forth (Keynes, 1936, p. 170).

This tripartite division of the forces underlying the demand for money calls for a few comments.

In the first place, what Keynes intends to do here is clearly to present a classification of various purposes money may serve. 'Motives' are a misnomer. We are engaged in the field of praxeology, not psychology. Secondly, we can see no obvious reason why speculators, even 'bears', should demand money. The obvious forms in which to hold their wealth would appear to be short-term interest-bearing financial assets, such as bills. Oddly, in the *Treatise* Keynes had admitted this 'since professional investors have other, and generally more profitable, means of lending bear funds against liquid claims on cash than through the Banking System, e.g. by buying Treasury Bills and by direct loans to the Money Market and the Stock Exchange' (p. 252). So there does not seem to be much scope for a 'speculative demand' for money, possible fluctuations in which might jeopardise the supply of money for business transactions. It appears that we have to rely mainly on the 'precautionary demand' for money, i.e. the demand for money as a reserve asset, to find a rival for the transactions demand.

Thirdly, although expectations make their formal appearance in the *General Theory*, Keynes treats them throughout in a rather haphazard fashion. They affect marginal efficiency of capital, liquidity preference and user cost, but not the marginal propensity to consume and, hence, not the magnitude of the multiplier. In an age of consumer credit this sounds odd. It is hard to avoid the conclusion that Keynes introduces expectations when they suit his argument, and leaves them out when they do not. The main purpose of the *General Theory* is to entrench the 'principle of effective demand'. Everything else, including expectations, is a means to this end.

True as all this may be, we have so far remained close to the surface of the argument Keynes conducted. The roots of his subjectivism lie much deeper. In 1965 Shackle was the first to draw our attention to the real problem involved here:

> There is an arresting contrast between the method and the meaning of Keynes' book. The method is the analysis of equilibrium, the endeavour to account for men's actions as a rational, calculated and logically justifiable response to circumstances which in all relevant essentials they thoroughly know. The meaning is that such rationality is in the nature of things impossible and baseless, because men confront an unknown and unknowable future (Shackle, 1965, p. 44).

Since then a fairly wide agreement appears to have been reached that Keynes' 'real opinion' on the significance of uncertainty for economic action is to be found not in the *General Theory*, but in his famous article in the *Quarterly Journal of Economics*, February 1937. Here Keynes explains that by 'uncertain' knowledge,

> I do not mean merely to distinguish what is known for certain from what is only probable. The game of roulette is not subject, in this sense, to uncertainty; nor is the prospect of a Victory Bond being drawn. Or again, the expectation of life is only slightly uncertain. Even the weather is only moderately uncertain. The sense in which I am using the term is that in which the prospect of a European war is uncertain or the price of copper and the rate of interest twenty years hence, or the obsolescence of a new invention, or the position of private wealth-owners in the social system in 1970. About these matters there is no scientific basis on which

to form any capable probability whatever. We simply do not know (Keynes, 1937 in S. E. Harris, 1947, p. 185).

This, then, appears to mark the latest (and highest?) stage of Keynesian subjectivism. It calls for three observations. In the first place, Keynes here draws a clear line of distinction between risk and uncertainty, between future events concerning which we are capable of forming probability judgments and those concerning which we are incapable of doing so. Hence, macroeconomists who in later years have attempted to blur this line of distinction can lay no claim to the title of 'Keynesians'.

Secondly, we now learn why it is impossible to regard human action concerned with the future, a category comprehending all economic action, as mere reaction to present events. Expectations, however formed, have to be given a place in the description of such action, and these expectations must not be treated as purely adaptive: they may change without any observable change in present circumstances. The point is germane to what we called above the 'second strand' of the thrust towards subjectivism, that is, the distinction between action and reaction, and the refusal to regard the shifting stances and postures of agile minds confronting an unknowable future as nothing but 'responses to opportunities', observable at least to them if not to all, and emanating from a supposed set of 'dispositions'.

Following on from what Keynes says, it is, for instance, clearly impossible to regard the amount of annual investment as a function of the rate of interest without taking account of probably shifting, and almost inevitably divergent, expectations. In the light of this conclusion the ISLM model and all similar conceptions stand condemned as misconceived. In fact there can be no such thing as an IS curve constant at least for the 'short period'. It shifts every time the state of expectations changes. The argument permits us to draw a general conclusion even more far-reaching and significant. As action is not the same thing as reaction it is impossible to let action appear in the conceptual form of a system of functional relationships in which at least several functions are designed to depict human reaction to given circumstances. In planning and acting our mind always has to take account of some circumstances that are by no means 'given' to it.

Thirdly, however, there arises the question whether expectations, if of such importance, might not be made at least more amenable to quantification by introducing them into a system of functional relationships as a set of independent variables. Apparently at some stage this is what Keynes had intended to do.

> In an early draft of the *General Theory* the consumption and investment functions contained an explicit variable, E, to represent the state of long-term expectations which were independent of the system, such that a stochastic change in E could shift the entire functional relation. Only with E assumed given and constant at some particular level could the functions be assumed constant (Kregel, 1976, p. 211).

Why did Keynes abandon this approach in the final version of his *General Theory*? Professor Kregel's explanation – 'But such a picture with unpredictable shifting functions and unforeseen change was ill suited to the exposition of what Keynes felt to be his most fundamental contribution, the principle of effective demand' – tallies with our own interpretation that in the *General Theory* expectations were to him essentially a means to an end, to be used or discarded as they suited his (mostly polemical) purpose.

If expectations, that is, thoughts about the future, matter, how are they to be given a satisfactory conceptual form? Only individuals can hold expectations. A 'state of expectations' as a macroeconomic variable must either mean a state of affairs in which all members of a trading community hold identical expectations, and such a state can hardly exist, or a constellation of divergent expectations, in which case aggregation is impossible. We can scarcely believe that, for example, bullish and bearish expectations will mostly move in such 'random fashion' as to offset each other. The plain fact is that not a day can pass without some trader changing one of his expectations. Whatever he does thereupon must, directly or indirectly, affect the expectations held by others. (In a situation in which some minds have an impact on other minds there is no scope at all for 'random forces'.) Hence the 'state of expectations' must change every day. The 'short period' becomes compressed to a 'market day'. The 'state of expectations' as an independent variable of a short-period macroeconomic equilibrium model stands revealed as a praxeological misconception.

V

In the last 30 years we have witnessed a revival of the quantity theory. In its new garb it is commonly referred to as 'Monetarism'. In this process of transformation one of the oldest macroeconomic doctrines, a relic of classical plutology, as we noticed earlier on, underwent in our time, we should be surprised to detect traces of the thrust toward subjectivism. In fact, even here we find some manifestations of it. It is of some significance, however, that, as we shall learn, these are confined to the first and third strands of our subjectivist skein of thought, to individual action and expectations. The second strand, connoting an emphasis on action rather than mere reaction to events, will be found lacking.

The main difference between the new quantity theory and the old is to be found in the fact that its main emphasis has shifted from M, the supply of money, to the demand for money and the function in which it is expressed. It is possible to feel of course that in making this move Professor Friedman, the distinguished architect of the edifice of the new quantity theory, was responding to the Keynesian challenge. He knew only too well that the success of his new version of an old theory of money would have to depend on his ability to present to the world something superior to liquidity preference. He had to meet Keynes on his own ground. It certainly is a mark of the success of Keynes's subjectivism that even his strongest opponent was forced to adopt it in order to defeat other Keynesian doctrines.

In his Equation (7) Friedman presents what he describes as 'the following demand function for money for an individual wealth holder':

$$\frac{M}{P} = f\ (y,\ w;\ r_m,\ r_b,\ r_e,\ \frac{1}{P}\frac{dP}{dt};\ u)$$

where M, P and y denote the holding of money, price level of goods and real income of a single wealth holder, and

w is the fraction of wealth in nonhuman form (or, alternatively, the fraction of income derived from property); r_m is the expected nominal rate of return on money; r_b is the expected nominal rate of return on fixed-value securities, including expected changes in their prices; r_e is the expected nominal rate of return on equities, including expected changes in their prices; $(\frac{1}{P}\frac{dP}{dt})$ is the expected rate of change of prices of goods and hence the expected nominal rate of return on real assets; and u is a portmanteau symbol standing for whatever variables othe than income may affect the utility attached to the services of money (Gordon, 1974, p. 13).

We are then told that we may obtain an equation that may be 'regarded as applying to the community as a whole' if we aggregate all these equations applying to individual wealth holders.

We note that Equation (7) explicitly refers to individuals of whom of course no account was taken in the older versions of the quantity theory. A first step is thus taken in the general direction of subjectivism. We also note the almost embarrassing variety of expectations appearing in this equation's determinants. One almost gains the impression that, where expectations are concerned, Friedman endeavours to outdo Keynes. This impression is not altogether deceptive. In his reply to Professor Davidson he says of his efforts that 'they extend the role of anticipations from the market for investments and loans, with which Keynes dealt, to a broader range of markets. In a respect that Davidson regards as distinctively Keynesian, therefore, my paper is more Keynesian than the *General Theory*!' (Gordon, 1974, p. 150). Considering the haphazard fashion in which Keynes treated expectations, Friedman here certainly scores a point!

At a first glance Equation (7) looks harmless enough. The variety of expectations the effects of which on the demand for money are traced here is, in a way, no less bewildering than it is impressive, while the inclusion of the portmanteau term u appears to deprive the exercise of much practical use. It is the context in which it appears that gives cause for concern.

We have to remember that Friedman's equations all form part of a system of functional relationships, that is, a general equilibrium model. Friedman tells us that

> the central idea I shall use in sketching the direction in which such a theory might be developed is the distinction between actual and anticipated magnitudes or . . . between measured and permanent magnitudes. At a long-run equilibrium position, all anticipations are realized, so that actual and anticipated magnitudes, or measured and permanent magnitudes, are equal.
>
> I shall regard long-run equilibrium as determined by the earlier quantity-theory model plus the Walrasian equations of general equilibrium. In a full statement, the earlier model should be expanded by including wealth in the consumption and liquidity preference functions, and the capital stock in the investment function, and by allowing for steady growth in output and prices (Gordon, 1974, pp. 48–9).

In his reply to Davidson, Friedman comments as follows on the passage just quoted:

The long-run equilibrium in which, as I put it, 'all anticipations are realized' and that is determined by 'the earlier quantity-theory plus the Walrasian equations of general equilibrium' is not a state that is assumed ever to be attained in practice. It is a logical construct that defines the norm or trend from which the actual world is always deviating but to which it is tending to return or about which it tends to fluctuate. The hypothesis that the logical construct does specify the norm or trend in this sense is entirely compatible with the existence of uncertainty, just as the hypothesis that $s = \frac{1}{2} gt^2$ specifies the law of falling bodies is entirely compatible with the existence of air. This does not mean that the hypothesis is correct. That is a question of fact to be determined by the consistency of the hypothesis with experience (ibid., p. 150).

In a footnote appended to the passage last quoted we are told:

But the relevant issue is not whether there are false trades and disappointments but whether such false trades and disappointments are 'sufficiently' important to change 'significantly' the trend about which the observed magnitudes fluctuate, or instead tend to be of the nature of random disturbances that largely average out over time. The answer need not of course be the same for all problems or under all circumstances. Unfortunately, armchair reasoning cannot settle such issues (ibid., p. 150, n. 13).

It is not our task to examine, or even to interpret, the views set forth in these passages. Naturally we are surprised to find that in an argument designed to apply Walrasian general equilibrium theory to the real world of unexpected change and growth, futures markets are never mentioned. Friedman's belief that the existence of uncertainty in the real world of action makes no more difference to the applicability of his theory than does the existence of air to that of a hypothesis formulated for vacuum conditions is, to say the least, intriguing. We may also wonder what effects divergent expectations held by individual wealth holders will have on the dependent variables of the system in equilibrium or disequilibrium. How do we aggregate divergent expectations as Equation (7) requires us to do?

Happily we need not concern ourselves with such weighty issues. Our concern here is solely with one aspect of the new quantity theory, namely, the thrust towards subjectivism. We noticed its impact in Equation (7) and found some evidence for a belief that here Friedman is emulating Keynes as a subjectivist. We now have to add that, if so, his success is limited. In the new quantity theory no trace is to be found of what we called earlier the second strand of subjectivism, the distinction between action and reaction. Friedman's system essentially is a system of functional relationships reflecting mostly reaction functions. In disequilibrium, we are told, 'the rate of adjustment in a variable is a function of the discrepancy between the measured and the anticipated value of that variable or its rate of change, as well as, perhaps, of other variables' (ibid., p. 48). There is no action, only reaction.[3] For reasons not for us to fathom Professor Friedman chose to don the mantle of a subjectivist. For reasons more readily understood he decided to borrow one from the Keynesian wardrobe. Embarrassing as it is, we cannot fail to notice how ill the garment fits him.

VI

In the first two sections of this chapter we presented an outline of the *modus operandi* of the modern credit economy with emphasis on the concurrence of minds which is its basis as well as on the disequilibrating forces it is apt to engender. In later sections we noted how the rise of this economy was accompanied by a general reorientation of monetary thought towards subjectivism.

The fact that in our world every day some lines of credit are opened, others closed, means of course that in some markets there is always some demand or supply not offset, as in a barter economy, by supply of or demand for another good. In other words, relative prices are continuously under pressure from such forces, although their strength and direction is continuously changing. In a world of General Equilibrium of course such pressures would not exist, or if they did, would soon subside.

The range of action of these forces is, however, by no means confined to the sphere of commodity markets and prices. The modern financial system contains a large number of markets for financial assets linked to the sources of credit creation in a number of ways. By an act of credit creation the borrower receives money while the lender is left with a financial asset which in most cases will be a negotiable instrument. While in general only such assets will be created as would find a ready market, the creation of each will have an effect on relative asset prices. (For all financial assets are links in a universal chain of substitutes.)

In a wealthy society there are many holders of portfolios. In most of them we would expect to find specimens of similar types of assets. Where this is so, such assets are fairly close links in a chain of substitutes. The markets for them are likely to be sensitive to the disappearance of or increase in any of them. Their yields will be related and respond quickly to changes in expectations.

Beyond the financial sphere we find that of real capital assets. The main link between them are of course industrial equities which are both, financial assets and claims to shares in real capital combinations. The chain of substitutable assets becomes weaker as it extends from the centre to the periphery, from the financial core to the outer regions of the economic system in which time-consuming processes of production have to be organized and to be made to recur. Along the chain the links grow more tenuous.[4] Markets for durable capital goods, like buildings and machinery, are not daily markets as financial markets are. They function differently, and the goods traded on them are not necessarily substitutes as are financial assets. Technology often imposes limits on substitutability and sometimes prescribes modes of complementarity. The circumstances in which either seems profitable may change abruptly.

No doubt violent changes in the amount of liquid assets available at the financial core will have repercussions throughout the system and will ultimately extend to the real capital sphere.[5] Such processes consist of a number of stages. What will happen during each of them will depend *inter alia* on shifting constellations of expectations. The effects of changes less violent may peter out before they reach the real capital sphere.

Austrian economists were the first to perceive the dangers that may arise when the effects of money capital available all too freely begin to affect the sphere of real capital in which acts of substitution are not as readily reversible as in the financial sphere, and in which links of complementarity once forged may become virtually indissoluble. Although these problems are rarely mentioned in the products of the textbook industry, we have no reason to believe that these dangers are today of less importance than they were 50 years ago. In reopening the case we would benefit from the possession of analytical tools more varied and more sophisticated than were available then. We might also draw some benefit from ordinary hindsight.

Furthermore, the moment may have come for a further step in the direction of subjectivism in what has long been an Austrian domain.

It has never been a plausible assumption that men who had learned to handle combinations of real capital resources in the arduous market conditions surrounding such activity should, time and again, fall into the same trap and allow themselves to be goaded into acts of substitution which would be irreversible when things went wrong.[6] This assumption is plainly another instance of the confusion between action and reaction. It is better, and certainly would be more in accord with the spirit of subjectivism, to interpret business action, in the capital sphere as elsewhere, as the endeavour of forward-looking and problem-solving men to exploit (problematic) opportunities and stave off (possible) disaster rather than as a mere response to 'market signals'. Changes in interest rates no doubt provide prospects of opportunities for profit by asset substitution. In the real world these and their implications have to be weighed by thinking men.

NOTES

1 For purposes such as ours in this chapter Marget's monumental work *The Theory of Prices*, 2 vols., New York, 1938, 1940 remains indispensable despite the fact that the period covered ends with the 1930s.

   In defending traditional quantity theory against the Keynesian strictures Marget offers us such wealth and variety of interpretation of the former as to make us feel that, at least as regards the range of diversity of possible interpretations, the recent revival of the quantity theory has run true to form.

2 In Swedish economics expectations had played a part ever since the pupils of Wicksell found it impossible to interpret the heritage of their master without making use of them and finding some conceptual form in which to insert them into their models.

   For a somewhat different interpretation of the role of expectations in English economics see Kregel (1977).

3 By contrast, 'In Keynes's full view of the system it is the conjectural and often figmental state of human expectations which are the prime movers of a free enterprise economic system. Thus, in the Keynes paradigm, supply and demand functions exist at any point in time but they need not be stable over any length of historical time' (Davidson, 1978, p. 381).

4 What we say here is essentially an attempt to explore, and take a little further in an Austrian direction, the intriguing tripartite division of 'Core, Mantle and Industry' in Hicks (1977), pp. 75–9.

5 'If portfolios are to absorb greater quantities of money, prices of other assets – not just Treasury bills and corporate bonds but equities and used cars – must change, mostly rise. Increases in the values of existing stocks

of physical assets, or titles to physical assets, encourage the production of new goods of the same type or close substitutes (James Tobin, 'Postscript' in Gordon, 1974, p. 88).

6 For a first little skirmish on this subject, see Lachmann (1977), pp. 75–9, and Mises's comment on it in Mises (1943).

6

Markets and the Market

It is, I think, a further illustration of the appalling Scholasticism into which the minds of so many economists have got which allow them to take leave of their intuitions altogether. Yet in writing economics one is not writing a mathematical proof or a legal document. One is trying to arouse and appeal to the reader's intuitions; and if he has worked himself into a state where he has none, one is helpless!
(J. M. Keynes, Collected Writings, vol. XXIX, pp. 150–51)

I

It is instructive to compare the present situation of economic theory with that Schumpeter faced when, around 1910, he set out to write his 'Theory of Economic Development'. What is to us of some interest to observe is our different attitude to the relevance of the Walras-Paretian general equilibrium model to the reality of the capitalistic market economy, and the conclusions to be drawn from this fact.

Schumpeter, while a sincere admirer of the Walrasian achievement and, in his first German book, an able exponent of the Paretian version of it, clearly realized that certain important phenomena of the world of capitalism did not 'fit' into the general equilibrium model. He recognized that the economic forces operating within this model would not have been capable of giving birth to what he called 'economic development', that is, in our terminology, economic growth of the kind that took place in the world economy during the last hundred years. Perhaps just not naive enough to believe in the possibility of 'steady state growth' in a world in which durable and specific capital equipment had come to play such a prominent part, he clearly saw that no ordinary 'changes of data' could possibly have caused the various stages of industrial revolutions the world has gone through. He then extended the argument to various phenomena he regarded as cognate to such irregular growth, and not inherent in the circumstances of an 'evenly rotating economy' that might give rise to a state of general equilibrium. He included among these not merely the business cycle and the modern credit system, as well as all profits and most private investment, but even capital and interest. In his view, all these exist in our world because we are not living in a general equilibrium world. They are caused by the action of a class of men for whom there would be no place in the latter, but who are very much at home in ours, even when they are unsuccessful, that is, innovating entrepreneurs who create 'new combinations of resources', men of action and not merely of reaction. What distinguishes them from most of their fellow men is their ability to imagine future states of affairs and market circumstances which differ from those presently existing not just by marginal quantities, but which by quality and magnitude are completely different from them. Entrepreneurs, and only entrepreneurs, are capable of forming expectations of future circumstances altogether different from the present, and to act in accordance with them. In this respect, we are entitled to regard Schumpeter as a predecessor of Professor Shackle, who in recent years has done more than any other thinker to insist on the significance of the human imagination as a source of expectations.

How could Schumpeter reconcile his emphasis on 'creative destruction' as the function of the entrepreneur-innovator with his espousal of the general equilibrium framework? It would appear that he had, briefly, two answers to this question. On the one hand, while equilibrium belongs to the long run and equilibrating forces are thus typically long-run forces, operating gradually and slowly, each entrepreneur forms his new combinations and succeeds or fails with them in the short run. At any moment of course some entrepreneurs are active, but over successive short periods we find that they are always different people. For the profits of the innovator are essentially short-lived; in the long run they are wiped out by the forces of competition. Towards the end of his short spell of triumph the successful innovator finds himself surrounded by a host of imitators who trespass on his domain and whose activity begins to curtail his profits. Thus, in the end the long-run forces of competition wash over and destroy the position the entrepreneur-innovator had created for himself. In the long run all such profits vanish and profitless equilibrium is restored.

On the other hand, certain changes in the data of the equilibrium system could not be brought about except by entrepreneurial action, and their effects on the system will last, however short-lived the entrepreneurs' rewards may prove to be. Various possible forms of technical progress provide us with a good example.

'Learning by doing' as a form of technical progress is presumably within the reach of most producers. As a result, technical knowledge as a datum changes slowly and gradually, but continuously. But most of the major technical innovations which have transformed our world during the last two centuries were obviously not of this kind. Not merely were they accompanied by considerable shifts in data other than those pertaining to technical knowledge. It took in most cases several decades before their effects had percolated all sectors of the economic system. Economists of course have understood for a long time that for the general equilibrium model to be readily applicable to the real world changes in data have to be infrequent and of moderate magnitude, and the response of the dependent variables, prices and quantities of output, swift and decisive (their 'velocity of adjustment' high). So it seemed hard to see how the effect of major transformations could be made amenable to treatment within this framework.

Nevertheless, to ascribe to Schumpeter, writing around 1910, an awareness of difficulties which economists of the 1980s have come to take for granted, would be to commit an anachronism. The fact remains that for him entrepreneurial innovation was amenable to treatment within the general equilibrium framework. While certain major changes of data (without which our world would have remained in a stationary state) could only be brought about by men with a large store of unused energy and the willingness to face an uncertain future, in the long run the system absorbs the effects of entrepreneurial innovation and the forces of competition erode all profits. It is noteworthy here that the cause of major economic change is not to be found within the complex of functions that constitute our system, but outside it. For the explanation of economic progress, we might say, Schumpeter does not rely entirely on functional price theories, but finds it necessary to take recourse to 'genetic-causal' explanation with the location of the cause outside the general equilibrium system.

II

What can we hope to learn from a comparison of the present situation of economic theory with that Schumpeter faced more than seventy years ago? Historical comparison may serve many purposes. In the history of thought an idea may at one time illuminate an important feature of the real landscape, but at another time, the landscape having changed and the feature vanished, become an encumbrance which no longer has an unambiguous meaning and to which anybody may give whatever meaning he likes. The notion of value, by which classical economists meant the real measure of wealth in a world of permanently oscillating market prices, is a sad example of such an idea which has had its day and lost its pristine clarity.

Of one fact there can be little doubt. However many economic and social changes this century may have witnessed, entrepreneurial innovation has remained as much an indispensable ingredient of economic progress in the market economy of our time as it was at Schumpeter's. Also, like Schumpeter, we need a body of thought, to be obtained apparently only in the form of a theoretical model, which shows the interaction of innovating entrepreneurs with other economic forces. Here, Schumpeter confined his interest to interaction with equilibrating forces, a limitation justifiable from his point of view, since in an equilibrium model equilibrating forces must be major forces of overwhelming power; otherwise the continued existence of equilibrium is not vouchsafed. But we have today some reason to be more sceptical.

Today it is widely recognized that what has come to be called the 'Neo-Walrasian' equilibrium model has little to do with what happens in a typical capitalistic market economy of our time. We even have Professor Hahn's authority for such a view: 'It was, I believe, always understood that the equilibrium of Arrow–Debreu is not a description of an actual economy, and I have already given reasons why the concept should nonetheless be important and interesting. However, one certainly does want a conceptual apparatus which is much more nearly descriptive' (Hahn, 1973, p. 329).[1] The question then arises whether the erection of such an apparatus is at all possible on ground which has been selected in accordance with the axioms of the general equilibrium system.

There are of course many reasons why this model does not fit into our world. We mentioned already that changes of data would have to be few and far between, and the response to them of dependent variables instantaneous and complete. Moreover, in a capitalistic market economy there are stock exchanges and other asset markets, such as property markets, on which capital gains and losses are made every day. Hence the mode of the distribution of wealth (what in the technical language of modern economic theory is called 'initial endowments') changes every day. But this mode of distribution constitutes one of our data. Hence we have here a highly volatile datum. Even were we to assume constant preferences (a highly dubious assumption in a world in which new goods make their appearance every year) the fact that the holders of these preferences undergo continuous changes of their wealth means that the relevant market data change concomitantly. Since prices and outputs have to change every day in response to the changing demand data, how and when do we ever reach an equilibrium position?

Moreover, we are living in a world in which at least the prices of most industrial products, except those in second-hand markets, are fixprices and lack the flexibility required in a general equilibrium system. This means that there is no longer a 'price system' properly speaking. In this world output decisions, adjusting it to changes in demand, have mostly to be made without the benefit of the receipt of 'price signals'. Depressions no longer lead to lower prices, let alone wage rates. How all this came about, and what it entails for the operation of markets of various kinds, are questions to which we shall return later on in this chapter. Meanwhile we have to ask how and why modern economic theory came to adopt its present position, and why it seems so hard to move away from it, in particular, in Professor Hahn's phrase, in a 'descriptive' direction.

For a long time, ever since Walras and Pareto achieved their fame, and their style of thought was adopted by economists all over the world, there has been a discernible tendency to regard the attainment of one goal as the highest aim of economic theory, namely, determinateness of prices and outputs, the dependent variables of the equilibrium system. To this paramount aim much was sacrificed, in particular as regards realism of assumptions. For to ensure such determinateness it became necessary to formulate axioms and data of the economic system in such a way that the values of the dependent variables could be deduced from them by means of a few simple chains of logical reasoning or mathematical calculation. There is no room for ambiguity here. As a result, the independent variables of the system became more and more narrowly conceived and its axioms more and more absurd. Also, the need to safeguard determinate solutions became more and more reflected in the level of abstraction chosen. All phenomena whose emergence might interfere with the determinateness of prices and outputs had to be got rid of by abstracting from them. In other words, the ultimate triumph of the equilibrating forces was safeguarded by choosing levels of abstraction on which strong disequilibrating forces, or at least those that might cause trouble, do not exist. Of the resultant absurdity of this scheme of thought we shall give two examples.

Firstly, there is in it no longer any scope for the variety of human action. Instead of men who pursue a variety of ends by means more or less rational we only find 'agents' to whom rationality of action means nothing more than the maximization of some given function. We are told nothing at all about how agents became acquainted with these functions, or how changing knowledge would affect them, or what they would do if they came to doubt their permanent character. As an example of pointless abstraction (pointless, if we want to learn anything about human action) this transformation of acting men into 'agents', and of rationality into a mathematical operation can hardly be surpassed. A second example is the transformation the meaning of the word 'choice' has undergone in recent economic thought. In all languages known to us this word of course denotes a situation in which an actor faces a number of courses of action between which he has to *choose*, so that the outcome of his action cannot be known until he has made his choice. In other words, choice is the prototype of indeterminate action. The modern 'theory of choice', by contrast, which has to eschew indeterminateness at any cost, has made the word denote a situation in which, with given preferences and market prices, there literally *is nothing to choose*. By means of ingenious abstraction a word has been made to mean what it cannot mean!

Why this obsession with determinateness? To some extent, contemporary misapprehension, or rather too narrow an interpretation, of the meaning of 'scientific method' may have played a part. But it is also possible to feel that, while there once was a time when the quest for determinateness made sense, today it no longer does. In fact, we may say, the relevant change occurred more than a century ago.

From the age of Mercantilism to the 'subjective revolution' of the 1870s economics was generally regarded as the Science of Wealth, *plutology* as, following Hicks, we might call it. Political Economy, as it was known during most of the 19th century, was concerned with the nature and causes of the wealth of nations. Towards the end of the century, however, the focus of interest shifted to what, following Whately, Mises and Hicks, we might call *catallactics*, the study of the complex of relationships between millions of people in thousands of markets in a society in which division of labour has become universal. This was the original aim of Walras, while the Austrians strove for the same end in their own way.

As long as we pursue a practical purpose, such as maximizing the rate of increase of the wealth of our nation, we have to be sure that we have accounted for all the causal forces that, positively or negatively, might affect it. We then have to ascertain, in other words, that our object is fully determined by the causal forces under our control. Determinateness is simply a test of the success of our effort. With the rise of catallactics the need for such practical efforts fell away, and with it the need for the quest for determinateness. Walras unfortunately linked his catallactic purpose to a method which required determinateness as a criterion of success, and began to use the concept of equilibrium as a test of such determinateness, as his main analytical tool, on all the three levels of individual, market and system.

III

Before we start on the retreat from determinateness let us take our bearings. Our task is to allot to the innovating entrepreneur a place within the catallactic system of modern industrial society, not within the framework of the general equilibrium system. It is true that, if the study of catallactics involves the plans of action of millions of people in thousands of markets, there is implicit in the problem thus posed the notion of mutual orientation, the perception of the fact that to some extent all these plans must be attuned to each other. If so, they may all succeed while inconsistency of plans would spell failure. But the fact that, inherent within the whole range of constellations of plans which constitutes our field of study, there is just one point which signifies complete consistency of all these plans, in no way entitles us to make this exceptional case our standard case and to regard all other forms of constellations as 'deviations' from it. It would be even less admissible to regard this case as the only position in which the economic system finds itself in a state of rest, an equilibrium position, *a centre of gravitation*. For to attune our plans successfully to those of others would require that we *know* all these plans, quite apart from the fact that if some of these plans were inconsistent with each other our problem would become unmanageable. It is hard to see how such knowledge could be derived from ordinary market experience.

The task of economic theory, as of other social sciences, is to make the world of human action intelligible to us. This world offers little scope for determinism. Our aim is to understand why men, hence entrepreneurs, act in the way they do. All men seek to achieve ends by the use of means, but ends are usually problematic, even while they are 'given', while the suitability of the means we command, relative to other means we do not, but might perhaps acquire, is always problematic. Choice between alternative courses of action is a central problem of human action and requires for our comprehension of it a theory of choice. As we explained above, no theory of choice worth its name is compatible with determinism.

It is true that to trace the undesigned consequences of economic action has for a long time been regarded as one of the tasks of economic theory, if not its only task. But it has also been recognized for what is by now a fairly long time that, strictly speaking, this can be achieved only under fairly stringent *ceteris paribus* conditions, where expectations figure prominently among the *cetera* that have to remain *paria* for the duration of our enquiry. It is hard to see how expectations, fed by the continuous stream of the news, can remain constant for any significant stretch of time.

If the aim of our enquiry is to enable us to understand why men act in the way they do, we shall of course have to assume that their action, by and large, though not necessarily in each individual case, conforms to a universal, and thus recognizable pattern, that is, that of rational action. We wish to stress that we use this term here in its original commonsense meaning, and not in the sense it has of late come to acquire in the jargon of our contemporary textbook industry. Here rational action now means nothing more than the maximization of certain functions. We use the term in its traditional meaning of 'bringing reason and experience interpreted by reason to bear on one's circumstances'. Needless to say, rational action in this sense implies an attitude of critical scrutiny, rather than of headlong 'maximization', towards any function one happens to encounter.

On the road of the retreat from determinism we may expect the Austrian School of economics to come into its own again. From the start, members of this school have made it their task to explain human action and to espouse subjectivism. Of the three leaders of the 'subjective revolution' of the 1870s Menger alone was never committed to determinateness, while Jevons and Walras, each in his own way, were. While it is true that for him the main task of economics was the quest for 'exact laws', and thus determinate solutions *to them*, he certainly did not conceive of economic theory as a comprehensive network entailing a determinate magnitude for every price and output quantity. Areas in which the treasure of determinate solutions is to be found were to him little islands in an uncharted and tempestuous sea.

In Mises' words,

> What distinguishes the Austrian School and will lend it immortal fame is precisely the fact that it created a theory of economic action and not of economic equilibrium or non-action. The Austrian School, too, uses the idea of rest and equilibrium which economic thought cannot do without. But it is always aware of the purely instrumental nature of such an idea, and similar aids. The Austrian School endeavors to explain prices that are really paid in the market, and not just prices that would be paid under certain, never realizable conditions . . . It has never suffered from the illusion that values can be measured (Mises, 1978, p. 36).

As we said above, in a good deal of latter-day economics the need to safeguard determinate solutions was reflected in the level of abstraction chosen. On our road of retreat from determinateness, by contrast, we shall find it possible and often expedient to choose levels of abstraction that suit our purposes. We do not have to choose levels on which most disequilibrating forces vanish from sight. Often we shall find it expedient to reverse the process of abstraction recently indulged in and to draw distinctions significant for our purposes.

Entrepreneurs meet different circumstances in different markets. Accordingly we shall have to distinguish between types of markets. In general, markets, not the market, are our theme. Similarly, a world of function-maximizing 'agents' has little of interest to offer us. As soon as we realize that different men engage in different activities, and that even in the same activity some may be more 'active' than others, we are well on our way to understanding a world in which, more or less, men bring reason to bear upon their circumstances as they see them. The mere fact that Schumpeter found it necessary to introduce his 'entrepreneur', a rather special kind of agent, in order to give an account of the most significant happenings in a modern market economy bears out what we say. As regards disequilibrating forces, we of course have to do more than merely refrain from abstracting from them; we must make an attempt to understand the circumstances in which they matter.

As regards the distinctions to be introduced, we shall speak not just of agents, but of producers and traders, not just of entrepreneurs, but of innovators and speculators, not just of agents who passively react to market prices, but of price-takers and price-fixers (who may have different functions in different markets). Also, different agents in different markets may enjoy different ranges of action.

In the following section of this chapter we shall make use of three distinctions stemming from the Keynesian ambient. We shall distinguish between a production and an exchange economy, between a co-operative and an entrepreneur economy, and between a fixprice and flexprice economy. We shall make use of these notions since they are ready at hand, but we shall use them for our purposes, which are not those for which they were originally devised.[2] We shall, in particular, relate the innovating entrepreneur to these distinctions, but, quite apart from this, we shall find that their use enables us to elucidate a number of aspects of economic action which, while of obvious interest in an industrial market economy, are today as a rule ignored in economic theory. We hope to distil conclusions of some praxeological significance from material not originally collected for this purpose.

IV

Production economies (and models) differ from exchange economies (and models) by the possibility in the former, but not in the latter, of two potential uses of one's initial endowments and two ways of achieving one's desired final collection of goods and services; initial endowments may be used for their desired (final) utility either by their initial possessors or by those who buy or rent them; or they may be used by their original possessors or others, on instruments in the production of desired final goods. Final goods may be obtained by trade, if they are part of the initial endowments, or by the transformation process we call production.

The transformation process takes time. Exchange also takes time, as any frustrated shopper knows, but that can be put down to problems with 'logistics of exchange' which are in principle meliorable. The potential for reduction of shopping costs justifies the analysis of exchange as if it were instantaneous, while no such justification exists for production.

The demand for the input precedes the (expected) demand for the output: inputs and outputs are therefore not subject to the same budget restraint except by playing tricks with time (e.g. recontracting) (Chick, 1981, pp. 405–6).

From Dr Chick's incisive explanation of the terms of the distinction it should be clear that Schumpeter's innovating entrepreneur must be conceived of as operating within a production, not an exchange economy. He has to transform whatever combination of resources he may have at his disposal at any given point of time by way of 'initial endowment' into a collection of goods, capital or final goods, which will emerge at a later point of time. Or, perhaps, we may say that he uses the input stream flowing from his combination of resources in order to produce an output stream for which he expects a demand. In any case the process takes (irreversible) time and his input demand precedes the expected demand for his output. This is so even where the entrepreneurial activity consists in moving physically unchanged goods from one place to another, for example in export trade.

It is also clear now why the Schumpeterian entrepreneur does not fit into the Walrasian system. Though the latter appears to comprehend production as well as exchange activity, this is only apparently the case. For, as Dr Chick rightly observes, the introduction of recontract, whether in its Edgeworthian or its Walrasian form, effectively removes from the scene all the essential features of the production economy and thus turns it into a mere exchange economy. Producers who do not start their production processes before they have come to know all relevant input and output prices do not really operate in a production economy. We might therefore call the Walrasian system a false production economy.

But we can go farther and distil from our distinction conclusions of praxeological substance which undoubtedly were beyond the purview of the post-Keynesian economists who introduced it.

Production processes are guided by production plans. In each plan ends and means are coordinated and obstacles mapped. As ends always lie in the future, while means may be presently available to the planner or expected to become available at some later time, the plan must have a time dimension no less than the production process it guides. Each plan therefore rests on expectations which may or may not be fulfilled as it is carried out. From time to time it will have to be revised. At some time the plan may even turn out to be incapable of being carried out. Then a new plan has to be made and action guided by plan modified in accordance with it. Needless to say, the borderline between plan revision and the making of new plans is an entirely arbitrary one.

A plan is a web of thought which accompanies and guides observable action. We are able to understand the meaning of the latter in terms of the former. It goes without saying that the circumstance of this link between thought and action is a distinguishing feature of human action, without parallel in nature. It provides us with a clue to our understanding of the praxeological significance of production processes. The conceptual apparatus requisite for our appraisal of events in a production economy thus rests firmly on the notions of plan and planned action.

At this juncture it is of some interest to turn our minds to the neoclassical model and ask similar questions about the conceptual apparatus requisite to it. We find that the apparatus of plan and planned action does not fit it at all. A plan is a web of thought that may be put into practice or modified if certain events take place or fail to happen. A preference function to be maximized is evidently something altogether different. It serves the purpose of enabling us to move from one equilibrium position to another instantaneously when prices change. The planner has to act in an uncertain world: he may wish to rectify *ex post* decisions formerly made. The maximizer of given functions can rectify nothing, he can merely react to outside events.[3] If we wish to interpret the apparatus of preference functions in terms of plans we would have to say that individuals at some point of time (in their puberty?) make such a large number of alternative plans that all possibilities that might arise during their active life-time are fully covered!

In a timeless exchange economy in which, as it were, 'everything happens at once' the conceptual apparatus of plan and planned action is not merely not needed, it would constitute an actual embarrassment since it does not fit into this environment. But time-consuming production processes are a prominent feature of the world in which we live, and the legitimacy of employing a conceptual apparatus which offers no scope for modifiable production plans (except within the artificial precincts of *tâtonnement*) in order to depict such a world must be open to serious doubt. It seems that a major revision of the conceptual structure of economic theory is now called for.

We now turn to considering the implications of the distinction between a cooperative and an entrepreneur economy, which Keynes introduced in a 1933 draft of the *General Theory* but later abandoned (J. M. Keynes, *Collected Writings*, vol. XXIX, pp. 76ff.).

Keynes introduces the distinction in the following way:

> The Classical Economics presupposes that the factors of production desire and receive as the reward of their efforts nothing but a

predetermined share of the aggregate output of all kinds which they can produce, both the demand and the supply of each factor depending upon the expected amount of their reward in terms of output in general. . . . The essential point is that by whatever roundabout methods every factor of production ultimately accepts as its reward a predetermined share of the expected current output either in kind or in terms of something which has an exchange value equal to that of the predetermined share (pp. 76–7).

We can then distinguish three types of society, of which the first conforms exactly to the pattern just described while the two others are to be characterized by their difference from it.

The first type of society we will call a *real-wage* or *cooperative economy*. The second type, in which the factors are hired by entrepreneurs for money but where there is a mechanism of some kind to ensure that the exchange value of the money incomes of the factors is always equal in the aggregate to the proportion of current output which would have been the factors' share in a cooperative economy, we will call a *neutral entrepreneur economy*, or a *neutral economy* for short. The third type, of which the second is a limiting case, in which the entrepreneurs hire the factors for money, but without such a mechanism as the above, we will call a *money-wage* or *entrepreneur economy* . . . It is obvious on these definitions that it is in an entrepreneur economy that we actually live to-day.

The law of production in an entrepreneur economy can be stated as follows: A process of production will not be started up, unless the money proceeds expected from the sale of the output are at least equal to the money costs which could be avoided by not starting up the process (ibid., pp. 77–8).

Obviously, we have to be on our guard against a confusion that may here arise from different uses of the word *entrepreneur*. While to Keynes the word denotes anybody who hires factors of production, to Schumpeter the entrepreneur is an innovator, an initiator of new combinations of factors. Nonetheless, there is a significant affinity between both thinkers: to both of them a range of action of different width is open to different agents, and the notion of the entrepreneur serves in both cases to delineate a class of agents to whom a wider range is open than to other people. For Keynes it is entrepreneurs who initiate production processes and hire factors of production by money contracts. A cooperative production economy is conceivable, but modern industrial society is not of this type.

To Keynes what mattered most here was of course that these money contracts provided a floor to industrial prices. Without stability of the latter, at least in the short run, these contracts would impose an intolerable burden. Wage earners, on their part, face a fairly narrow range of economic action: they cannot bargain for real earnings, their bargaining capacity is confined to the determination of money wages. The unemployed as individuals, moreover, (and whatever they might achieve when organized) are unable to induce an employer to hire them by offering him terms more favourable than those granted to those he presently employs. In modern reality of course, the terms of the labour contract are typically agreed upon by employers' representatives and trade union officials, and thus are beyond the reach of any individual, employer or worker.

This narrowing of the range of action confronting individuals is a phenomenon by no means confined to the modern labour market. It has become fairly typical of markets for consumer goods in our world generally. The modern consumer, on entering a department or chain store, confronts a range of goods each of which has a price tag attached to it. All he or she is able to do is to make a choice between them in accordance with preferences and budget constraint. Prices and qualities of the goods on offer are literally 'given' to him or her. Any attempt to vary them by negotiation would be utterly futile.

From a historical perspective, this is quite a recent phenomenon. Few economists appear to be aware how novel it really is. Over the centuries, all over the world, market dealings have taken place among 'higgling and bargaining' between buyers and sellers. In many parts of the world, typically of course in its less developed regions, it is still the case today. In many European countries, less than a century ago, housewives buying food from peasant producers who brought it to town on market days would spend a good deal of their time haggling about prices. 'Fixprices' were then unknown, at least in such markets. In this world almost everybody, whether buyer or seller, contributed to the making of market prices, was at least a potential pricemaker. In so far as the restriction of the pricemaking function to a minority of agents bears on the rise of fixprice markets in our world, this phenomenon will be considered further below. It is not only with regard to participation in pricemaking, however, that the consumer's range of action has been narrowed. As long as dresses, suits and shoes were made to a customer's order, the latter participated in the production process by exercising his choice as regards style, number of buttons and pockets, etc. Nowadays the only choice the customer has is between a number of finished products. He is excluded from the production process and confined to an exchange economy.

The cause of this development lies of course in cost economies. Time saved in higgling and bargaining can more profitably be used elsewhere. Standardization of products permits the utilization of economies of scale. Even though there is always the danger that the standardized products will find few buyers, this development may be worth while, even to those whose range of action is thus restricted. Of course they have no say in the matter.

To our innovating entrepreneurs the development must have been a boon. Quite apart from the fact that in our world no employer would be able to negotiate with each employee separately on conditions of employment, it enabled him to save time and effort for the tasks that matter.[4]

V

The conclusions of wider praxeological significance that matter to us are these: in the first place, in our world different classes of agents typically face limited ranges of action with different limits. In different markets, different classes of such agents confront each other, for example in asset and consumer goods markets. Hence the market processes engendered in such markets will be affected by these differences. It is, in general, wiser to speak of *markets* rather than of *the market*.

Secondly, as is by now well known, in the absence of recontract the equilibrium position finally reached must depend on the events that took place on the 'path' towards it, and 'false trading' will have the effect of modifying some of the 'data'. We now have to add that what happens on this 'path' will also depend on the limits imposed on the ranges of action open to the various classes of agents engaged in these transactions. These limits are in effect also limits on the strength of the equilibrating forces.

We now come to deal with the third of our distinctions, that between fixprice and flexprice markets. As is by now widely known, the significant difference between them does not lie in the fact that in the latter prices move while in the former they do not, but in the fact that in the latter prices move under the impact of supply and demand, while in the former they move in accordance with criteria regarded as relevant by the pricefixers. In a flexprice market everybody is, at least potentially, a pricemaker, in a fixprice market there is only one pricemaker, and he need not be a participant in the market, a 'trader', but may exercise his authority from outside the market.

The evolution of fixprice markets has been a typical feature of our time. How does the innovating entrepreneur cope with this new situation not envisaged by Schumpeter? It seems that, on the whole, entrepreneurs have managed well enough. In many ways it is of course an advantage to be able to fix the prices of the goods one sells rather than have them determined by anonymous forces in a market one is unable to influence. But of course this does not mean that our entrepreneur no longer has to contend with competitors. The force of competition is now reflected in quantities of goods sold rather than in prices obtained. Competition still causes the erosion of profits. Our entrepreneur, when finding the market for his product surrounded by an array of close substitutes, may now take evasive action by means of differentiating his product from them.

As we said above, the rise of fixprice markets has been a typical feature of our time. In particular, markets for industrial products are today predominantly of this type. What were the reasons for this development?

Sir John Hicks believes that

> One of them . . . is the increasing scope of large-scale economies – the 'growth in the size of the firm' – which itself makes the atomistic type of market harder to operate. Another . . . is standardisation (branding and packaging), the ability of the producer, using modern technology, to give a quality imprint. Standardisation of quality, and standardisation of price, have a strong inclination to go together . . . It is a consequence of the standardisation that the role of the merchant is diminished (Hicks, 1977, p. xi).

This last point needs some emphasis. In the Victorian era the typical pricemaker in markets for industrial goods, say hardware or textiles, was the wholesale merchant. As we pointed out some years ago,

> Here was a broker whose interest was primarily in maximizing turnover, and who could therefore be relied upon to offer manufacturers and

charge retailers such prices as would enable him to accomplish this aim. . . . Here, in short, was a 'middleman' whose economic function was not so much to 'distribute goods' as to collect and impart information and to fix such prices as would maximize his turnover. And such prices evidently had to be flexible! (Lachmann, 1956, p. 64).

In our world the wholesale merchant as a pricemaker has been succeeded by the industrial cost accountant whose orientation is altogether different. For him, apparently, size of turnover, while of course never to be ignored, takes second place after the maintenance of a satisfactory price–cost margin. In our world a fall in demand for industrial goods does not, in general, cause a fall in their prices, but a fall in output and employment. We also have to bear in mind that for any merchant to be engaged in trading at flexible prices his turnover must be large enough to make such activity worth while as a fulltime occupation, while to the industrial cost accountant pricefixing need be no more than a part-time occupation.

In assessing the praxeological significance of the conclusions to be drawn from the introduction of our three distinctions we notice, first of all, limitations on the range of choice faced by agents which are not dreamt of in neoclassical philosophy. But while the number of pricemakers has diminished, the range of action open to manufacturers is enhanced: they have taken over the pricefixing function from merchants. In our world flexible prices have become a characteristic of financial asset markets and large raw material markets. Although consumer goods markets (except for second-hand markets) are now largely fixprice markets, we should resist the temptation to identify fixprices with the production economy and flexprices with the exchange economy. There is, however, no doubt that the evolution of fixprices constituted a response to the needs of the modern production economy. In a flexprice market it is impossible to send out price lists to customers.

Our main conclusions are, in the first place, that different markets, characterized by the encounter of different classes of agents with different interests and functions, will give rise to market processes of various kinds. In the light of this insight all statements suggesting that *the market* will produce this or that result must be regarded with some suspicion. It is better to speak of *markets* than of *the market*. Our assessment of the relative strength of equilibrating and disequilibrating market forces must, in each instance, take account of the facts enumerated.

Our second conclusion is that, if a conceptual apparatus offering scope for planning and planned action is necessary in order to enable us to give an account of the working of a production economy, since production is guided by plans and cannot be understood without reference to them, it is equally necessary in order to permit us to grasp the *modus operandi* of any economic activity whatsoever. A major revision of the foundations of economic theory with more emphasis on planned action and less emphasis on mere reaction to changing circumstances (movements along given indifference curves) appears to be called for.

VI

On our road of retreat from determinism we found it expedient to introduce a few distinctions germane to forms of action and classes of agents for which there is no place in the realm of neoclassical orthodoxy. Moving on a level of abstraction lower than that dictated by the need to ensure the overwhelming strength of equilibrating forces at all costs, we were able to make use of some conceptual differences which permitted us to open new vistas on the world of real markets, vistas which were apparently beyond the purview of those economists who first drew our attention to these differences.

We now have to add another distinction that concerns classes of entrepreneurs. If we want to be able to disentangle the complex skein of interaction between equilibrating and disequilibrating forces, no longer taking for granted the invariable supremacy of the former, we need a classification of types of entrepreneurs of such a kind that relevant distinctions here are reflected in different modes of interaction there.

A threefold scheme of classification is suggested by experience as well as our analytical needs: (1) arbitrageurs; (2) speculators; and (3) innovators.

While arbitrageurs make gains from existing price differences, or price-cost differences, speculators as well as innovators hope to make gains from intertemporal price differences or price-cost differences. But while the speculator merely hopes for such differences to come into existence as a result of developments over which he has no control (e.g. changes in demand or the size of harvests), the innovator hopes to bring about such profitable changes *by his own action*. While there may be scope for arbitrage even in a stationary world as a result of temporary changes, both speculators and innovators have to act on expectations, but the innovator's expectations are part of his production plan. The arbitrageur is of course always an equilibrating agent, the innovator a disequilibrating one, while the outcome of speculation depends on circumstances.

For Schumpeter the market processes engendered by the action of his innovators, whose profits were (in the long run) eroded by competition, were evidently propelled by interaction between entrepreneurs of our first and third category. Arbitrageurs exploiting new opportunities which owed their existence to innovation, successful or unsuccessful, would wipe them out by the very act of exploiting them. Speculation was of no interest to him, owing probably to its short-run character.

For us, by contrast, the outcome of market processes impelled by interaction between innovators and speculators is a subject we dare not ignore as our field of study is not surrounded by ditches designed to keep out all disequilibrating forces. Even if it could be shown that all speculation is ultimately an equilibrating force the possibility that speculators' successes and failures might affect some of the 'data' on the path towards equilibrium could not be ignored. We have to ask what happens if each innovator finds himself surrounded by a swarm of speculators trying to anticipate the outcome of his action. Will it tend to make his task easier or more difficult, make his days of success longer or shorter?

There is no simple answer to these questions. The outcome appears to depend on the exact form of the speculative activity involved.[5] A few examples will suffice to illustrate this conclusion. A speculator who buys stock in the innovator's company helps the latter, but one who buys stock in a business competing with his will help to reduce his profits. Where the innovation consists in the construction of a new railroad, those who buy land adjacent to the new line in order to become its customers help the project, but those who buy it to make capital gains from those who will want to become customers in the future, but meanwhile use the land for other purposes, make it more difficult. In general, where speculators are willing to hold variable stocks of what the innovator produces as output or requires as input, they may make it easier for him as long as they stand ready to absorb or discharge differences between output flow and flow demand for it, or flow supply of input and the demand for it. But of course if they accumulate or unload their stocks at the wrong moment, i.e. in such fashion as to add to an excess of flow supply of output over its flow demand, or flow demand for input over its flow supply, they make the innovator's task harder.

If our innovator is pursued by a host of imitators ready to take evasive action into product variation, and if these imitators are, then, surrounded by swarms of speculators, very little can be said about the outcome of such market processes. As was explained in chapter 1 (p. 16), 'market processes consist of two phases succeeding each other in continuous iteration, which we may respectively describe as competition in the narrower sense and product variation. . . . We observe an alternation of two trends, a narrowing and a widening of the range of variety among products on the market. Innovation is followed by competition followed by the secondary innovations of product variation.' In either phase speculative activity may help or hinder the action of the other agents.

VII

In the following section we shall return to the problem of the predominant forces in fixprice and flexprice markets, but before doing so, let us first look at this whole field from a perspective which permits us to ask questions about the identity and characteristic modes of action of price setters in modern markets, and at the same time to understand why such questions have for so long been almost entirely neglected, at least by all those immersed into the main stream of economic thought.

Above we learnt that 'in our world different classes of agents typically face limited ranges of action with different limits' (see section V). In all markets there are price takers and price setters, but their characteristics may differ widely from market to market. The purposes pursued by, and the general mode of orientation of, price setters in modern industrial fixprice markets evidently have to be regarded as special problems arising within a general theory of price setting. At present, with one or two exceptions, such a general theory, alas, does not seem to exist. Why?

Even the exceptions exist in somewhat fragmentary form. We find them in Sir John Hicks's recent work such as that mentioned above (from *A Theory of Economic History*, 1969, onwards) and in that of the Post-Keynesian school.[6] Empirical, as distinct from analytical, work on 'administered' prices of course goes back to the 1930s, to the writings of Gardiner Means in the USA and to the enquiry set up by the Oxford Institute of Statistics in 1939.

Whether Keynes's *General Theory* has to be interpreted as assuming the prevalence of fixprices at least in markets for industrial products is a matter at present in dispute, with two such renowned interpreters as Dr Victoria Chick[7] and Sir John Hicks on opposite sides. Keynes himself of course never made this assumption *explicitly*. In emphasizing that workers are unable to determine their real wages by bargaining for them he must have assumed prices of wage goods to be flexible. He can hardly have thought that, in Britain in the 1930s, all wage goods were agricultural products.

Post-Keynesians, in stressing the importance of fixprices based on a 'mark-up' on wage costs, in modern industrial markets, have certainly gone beyond their master's words. Whether they have still kept within his meaning is one of the open questions related to their inheritance.

Outside the ranks of the Post-Keynesians we find an astonishing lack of curiosity about price setting, about the identity and modes of conduct of price setters. This puzzling state of affairs in a discipline almost all of whose members profess, and always have professed, a profound concern with markets and prices, calls for examination.

Every market transaction consists of offer and acceptance. Since no offer to sell or buy can be made without quoting a price, whoever makes an offer is a price setter. The crux of the matter lies in the fact, as stated in section V above, that even within the framework of equilibrium theory, the equilibrium position finally reached will depend on the 'path' towards it and 'false trading' will cause some modification of the 'data'. Also, what happens on this 'path' will *inter alia* depend on the limits imposed on the ranges of action open to the various classes of agents engaged in these transactions. In other words, it matters who sets prices and who takes them. *A fortiori*, if we abandon the notion of equilibrium and think in terms of market processes instead, when we no longer have a criterion of 'false' or 'right' trading, any act of price setting may have consequences stretching over an indefinite and indefinable period of time.

Neglect of price setting may be justified in market conditions in which either, whatever opening bids are and whoever makes them, we may expect their effects to be entirely wiped out by later events, or in which any agent, if need be, is able to turn price setter. The former is of course the well-known case of Edgeworthian *recontract* or Walrasian *tâtonnement*. It has no place in the real world. The latter would be a case in which all agents face (approximately) identical ranges of action so far as price setting is concerned. As we shall learn later on, such a condition actually does obtain in merchants' markets in which merchants are able to turn buyers or sellers, price setters or takers, as the market situation and their plans geared to it may require. Outside merchants' markets, however, such a condition is rarely to be found.

It is not to be denied that the neglect we complain about has its limits. No one, to our knowledge, ever doubted that in a monopolistic market the monopolist will be the price setter, nor that under oligopoly the various oligopolists are price setters with each taking his orientation from what prices he expects his rivals to set. It also is worth recording that, outside the precincts of the textbook industry at least, a good many economists have felt distinctly uneasy when they discovered that in a 'state of perfect competition' all agents are price takers and there is no visible price setter at all. For us, however, there is little comfort in such events. The discussions to which they ought to have given rise never took place.

It is of some interest to us to observe how various schools of economic thought other than the Post-Keynesians have responded to our problem. We shall consider in turn how classical, neoclassical and Austrian economists have come to grapple with it.

Classical economics encounters the problem of price setting in terms of its distinction between fluctuating market prices and values determined by cost of production. Value serves as the centre of gravitation of the range of fluctuations of the former. Whatever market prices are set, their effects will soon be nullified by the forces of gravitation. The classical case thus coincides with the first of the two cases examined above in which neglect of price setting appears to be justifiable.

We have to remember, though, that classical economics envisages a market in which every trader knows the value, that is, the long-run cost of production, of the commodity traded, and is therefore able to use this knowledge as his point of orientation for market action: whenever market price falls below this level he buys and vice versa. In these circumstances it is true that every market price emits a signal: it shows 'how far away from home' we are, where general knowledge of the geographical position of 'home' is taken for granted. Where this is no longer so, matters become more complex.

The importance of price setting for neoclassical economics evidently depends on whether we assume the existence of a universal 'auctioneer'. If he exists he nullifies all prices set prior to his coming into action, and the neglect of price setting seems justifiable. Otherwise, as we saw above, price setting problems will arise on the 'path' to equilibrium, in particular with false trading.

There may, however, be other cases in which neglect of our problem is to be justified. We know already that this will be so in conditions in which all agents face ranges of action that differ little. Perhaps we should also distinguish between normal and abnormal ranges of action. In markets with sudden excess demand or supply, it may happen that some unsatisfied buyers or sellers, though ordinarily price takers, turn price setters on realizing that otherwise they cannot get what they want. In fact, with strong excess demand this, sooner or later, is quite likely to happen. Perhaps this is the grain of commonsense meaning behind the excessive formalism of Professor Samuelson's Correspondence Principle which, at least as a general principle of dynamics in economic theory, many economists have greeted with reservations.

What matters to us is this: it is one thing to point to the possible occurrence of market situations in which the borderline between price takers and setters may become blurred as some of those who normally are price takers are induced to act as price setters instead. It is quite a different thing, however, to claim that this will always happen, and that we are thus entitled, in shaping our theory of markets, to abstract from this distinction altogether and to proceed as though in all markets all agents faced identical ranges of action.

What do Austrian economists have to say about these matters? We know of no modern Austrian discussion of the relations between price setters and takers within markets. In view of the fact that prominent Austrians have dubbed neoclassical price theories inadequate in being merely 'functional', and lacking the 'causal-genetic' quality of a true theory of price formation, this is a rather odd situation. When Mayer in 1932, in his well-known essay on 'The cognitive value of functional price theories' (*Der Erkenntiswert der funktionellen Preistheorien*) presented the criticisms mentioned, he certainly implied that the formulation of a causal-genetic theory of price formation was an urgent task for Austrian theory. And in his contribution to the Festschrift for Camillo Supino (*'Die Wert- und Preisbildung der Produktion-smittel'*) he explicitly stated that 'the essential cognitive aim of Austrian theory is the description of the actual process of price formation' (Mayer, 1930, p. 13), even though he had to admit that much, perhaps most, of the work remained to be done.[8]

In the quotation from his *Notes and Recollections* cited above, Mises fully endorsed this view of the task of Austrian theory. 'The Austrian

School endeavours to explain prices that are really paid in the market, and not just prices that would be paid under certain, never realizable conditions' (p. 123).

From a theory of price formation we are entitled to expect some information about the action of price formers. How, then, can we explain price formation without reference to the relations between price setters and takers? Do fixprice markets not constitute part of the object of such a theory? The lack of curiosity on the part of Austrian economists is even more astonishing than that of others.

Part of the explanation probably has to be sought in the fact that this Austrian theory of price formation, conceived like other Austrian ideas in the bright morning light of the early 1930s, has remained a project to this day. Nothing ever came of it. We may surmise that when the project is resumed the problem mentioned will have to be faced.

There may also be another explanation. It is all too easy to jump from the observation that competitive pressure erodes profits to the conclusion that *therefore* no earlier profit position can have lasting effects. Such an earlier position may of course have given rise to a chain of sequential changes while it lasted. (Malinvestment is the obvious example well known to Austrians.) And these sequential changes will often not be erased by the process of competition. To recognize the power of the competitive market process is important. Failure to recognize its limits may yet lead us astray. Austrian lack of curiosity about price setters and takers probably has one of its roots here.

VIII

From what we have just said it follows that if we wish to understand the significance of fixprice markets in general, and the mode of coexistence between fixprice and flexprice markets characteristic of our world in particular, such understanding will have to be sought within the framework of an 'Austrian type' theory of price formation, but on a level of abstraction sufficiently low to permit us to designate price setters and their ranges of action in various markets. While price formation may take many different forms, all market transactions consist of sequences of acts of offer and acceptance. Whoever makes an offer to sell or buy must make it in terms of price, i.e. in a money economy, of money price. All structural analysis of markets in their variety must start here, with the designation of price setters, with investigation of their identity and purposes, the ranges of action open to them and their typical modes of action within them.

As we stated above, in our world the flexprice type prevails in financial asset markets and those for raw materials, industrial and agricultural, while in modern industry, except in secondhand markets, the fixprice type predominates. For our better understanding of these phenomena, however, we have to make a distinction between *a salesman's* and *a merchant's market*.

Both salesman and merchant, to be sure, are economic agents deriving their incomes (commission, profit) from sales they try to maximize, but in doing so they have to take their bearings from different entities and their points of orientation lie in different directions.

The merchant buys and sells, i.e. he has to buy before he can sell; he must keep a stock. He can stay out of a market he deems unprofitable. For him the size of his stock is an important variable: he must neither 'run out of stock' as long as there is a prospect of profitable sale, nor see it pile up to unmanageable dimensions. The salesman, with a much narrower task, is not directly concerned with this, as within the organization that employs him this is not his function. (This does not mean that he is entirely exempt from possible consequences of such stock movements on his sales.)

The merchant *is a firm*, buying and selling, making plans for the profitable turnover of stock. The salesman is *part of a firm* which does these and other things. The salesman has his place at the end of a production flow, his function is to sell it. The merchant is concerned with turning over his stock which may or may not contain segments of output flows. It may be tempting to consign the merchant to an exchange economy, the salesman to a production economy, but we should resist this temptation. Grain and wine merchants deal in segments of production flows, and fairly complex structures of production may be required to sustain these.

In a merchant's market merchants may trade with other merchants or with non-merchant customers who may be either buyers or sellers, but a salesman's market requires customers who must be buyers. In a merchant's market a merchant may refuse another merchant's offer and counter it with a different offer of his own. In a salesman's market this is hardly possible. In a merchant's market a merchant may be price setter or price taker, and he may 'switch sides' between one day and the next. In a salesman's market nobody can do that.

In a merchant's market we must expect prices to be flexible, as there are so many potential price setters and any one of them may become active at any moment, for example if an offer, not necessarily made by or to him, is refused. A merchant can, and often has to, act on the spur of the moment. At any rate, the location of the price setter is within the market. In a salesman's market the price is normally set by somebody in the selling firm other than the salesman. In special cases of course concessions may be granted to important customers, but a salesman usually has to seek special authority to grant them. The price is here normally set outside the market. Price setting decisions are as a rule orientated to expected long-run circumstances.

Thus equipped we are now able to approach the vexed problem of 'market clearing prices'. In a trivial sense all markets may be said to 'clear' since sales must equal purchases. In a sense more germane to the actual issue we are concerned with we have to distinguish between the *ex ante* and *ex post* form of the problem. Excess demand or supply existing *ex ante* has to be eliminated by adjusting supply to demand, but this may be brought about by price or quantity adjustments. Marshall, to be sure, taught that in the short run prices, in the long run quantities, are the main forces causing the adjustment of market supply to demand, but this was a bold generalization, too bold probably even in Marshall's world, the world of British industrial markets in Victorian times, and much too bold for us. In our world the mode of adjustment differs from market to market, and our task now is to enquire whether the distinction between markets we introduced is germane to these differences of mode of adjustment.

There is good reason to believe that in a merchant's market prices will be flexible and the mode of price adjustment to changes in demand or supply will prevail. For it to be otherwise we would have to expect that merchants will maintain prices fixed even in the face of excess demand, i.e. that they will ignore a good chance of gain. With excess supply, on the other hand, merchants have to accumulate stock if they wish to maintain prices. This is a difficult thing to do for them, as for the regular accrual of profit they have to rely upon the regular turnover of their stock. Whatever upsets the time pattern planned will also upset other, complementary, plans. We have to remember that a merchant may deal in a number of goods and carry stocks of some or of each. When the rate of turnover of one of them is slowed down, he may miss profitable opportunities elsewhere. There may be an 'opportunity cost of waiting' here. Moreover, how will his creditors react to delay in the repayment of their loans?

In a salesman's market we encounter a situation altogether different. It is noteworthy that the cause of the difference lies not so much in the nature of the markets compared as in the character of the capital used in the production processes which ordinarily feed salesman's markets. The prominence of durable and specific capital equipment in the fixed capital of modern industry entails the absence of most of the problems just described which merchants trying to maintain prices have with the rate of turnover of their capital.

Everybody knows that in modern industry decisions to invest in fixed capital are virtually irreversible. 'Opportunity cost of waiting' finds its expression mainly in user cost. The rate of turnover of capital cannot be planned in advance. Everybody knows that in a world of fluctuating demand the rate of utilization of fixed capital will vary from year to year. The existence of some excess capacity is a normal feature of the situation and is taken for granted in decisions on depreciation of capital.

In such a situation price setters cannot take their orientation from the market scene shifting from day to day. Price setting therefore cannot be entrusted to salesmen. Price setters have to take their bearings from the need to keep the production process going. To safeguard the general pattern of complementarity of the segments of the output stream, in itself flexible in response to fluctuations in demand, becomes far more important than snatching ephemeral market opportunities. Salesmen's impulses may vary, but their superiors must beware of any urge to act on the spur of the moment if they want to serve the long-run interest of their firm. A merchant, by contrast, must learn to comply with this urge. Differences in mode of action often matter.[9]

Those who glibly speak of 'market clearing prices' tend to forget that over wide areas of modern markets it is not with this purpose in mind that prices are set. They seem unaware of the important insights into the process of price formation, an Austrian responsibility, of which they deprive themselves by clinging to a level of abstraction so high that on it most of what matters in the real world vanishes from sight.

The merchant embodies a style of action concerned with the exploitation of opportunities as they offer themselves in a kaleidic world. Profit is made on the turnover of working capital mobile between markets. As all markets are freely accessible this capital may take many forms varying over time. There are no modes of complementarity, technical or otherwise, to exercise constraint on the number of these forms, except that the merchant has to keep a cash balance in proportion to his turnover. In the language of the Post-Keynesian school the *axiom of gross substitution* holds here.[10] Only profitable opportunities and the availability of resources (including credit) set limits to action. The prototypical merchant activity is the carrying of stocks of agricultural commodities between harvesting time and the dates when consumers need them. Production and consumption dates are 'given', but even within these limits conditions may change considerably. As in a kaleidic world all opportunities lie in the future, all action by merchants is speculation.

In the course of the evolution of the capitalistic market economy the realm of the merchant has both shrunk and grown. The rise of modern industry has curtailed it, but the growth and increasing sophistication of financial asset markets has added new provinces to it. As all asset holders can, and in some circumstances would, sell their assets they are all potential merchants and the contents of all portfolios are, at least potentially, 'in the market'. As portfolios are revised these markets acquire their wellknown speculative character. They are merchant's markets whose special and characteristic feature is the continuous existence of immense stocks that might at any moment be 'thrown into the market'. Also, in this world, banks and similar institutions can no longer be regarded as simple intermediaries between lenders and borrowers, but have in effect become merchants whose stock consists of financial assets. They enjoy one remarkable advantage over commodity traders: as financial assets can be created and modified almost at will, by agreement between lender and borrower, they are, unlike wool merchants, not constrained by physical and technical limits.

The salesman's market, by contrast, belongs to a different world and the salesman embodies a different style of action. He is a member of a hierarchy, of an organization, typically the modern industrial firm in which largescale production takes place in accordance with complex long-run plans for production flows. The mode of organization is here that of bureaucracy. A large number of people cooperate, on the basis of division of labour, to produce an output stream which has to conform to a large number of requirements, technical, economic and otherwise. Men and women cooperating are organized in the form of a hierarchy in which orders and instructions issued by those in the higher have to be carried out by those in the lower echelons.

Experience has thus far shown this bureaucratic mode of organization to be the most efficient in the application of modern methods of mass production. It is a modern market institution which the market of course borrowed from the administrative and military organization of the modern state. (The market, we thus learn, need not evolve its own institutions. It may borrow them, if efficient, from other spheres of social life. This is not the place to pursue the implications.)

The overall production plan of the firm must give full expression to the complementarity of all the resources used, of the various types of labour and capital (fixed, working etc.). There is little scope here for the axiom of gross substitution. No abundance of lubricants will help us to overcome a shortage of electric energy. This plan must be flexible enough to permit fluctuations in demand to be met by supply adjustments. Complications may arise here from the irreversibility of investment in fixed capital. Excess capacity may be inevitable while other types of capital are adjustable to demand fluctuations.

In a bureaucratic hierarchy care has to be taken about the delimitation of spheres of competence, of ranges of action by officials. This is a corollary of the need for overall complementarity. While there must be no conflicts of competence, no activity must remain unassigned, otherwise there would be gaps in the pattern of complementarity. So salesmen and price setters have each their separate spheres of competence.

It will now be clear why, within a scheme of activity thus designed, nobody can be permitted to act on the spur of the moment. If any changes in it have to be made, they must be decided on by those at the top of the hierarchy, even though implemented by those in lower ranks.

In a salesman's market, even though salesmen must enjoy scope for initiative, with the scope carefully circumscribed, we can hardly expect prices to be adjusted frequently. Supply here has to be adjusted to demand directly, by quantity adjustment of output flow, within the framework of the overall plan but without the intermediary of price change.

NOTES

1 Of late Hahn has reiterated this view even more emphatically. 'I have always regarded Competitive General Equilibrium analysis as akin to the mock-up an aircraft engineer might build. My amazement in recent years has accordingly been very great to find that many economists are passing the mock-up off as an airworthy plane, and that politicians, bankers and

commentators are scrambling to get seats. This at a time when theorists all over the world have become aware that anything based on this mock-up is unlikely to fly, since it neglects some crucial aspects of the world, the recognition of which will force some drastic re-designing' (Hahn, 1981, p. 1036).

2   In the cases to be discussed Keynesian thinking is mainly concerned to show that in the world around us certain market forces do not and cannot operate as they are depicted in 'classical theory', while our aim is to *understand* the constellations of mental acts behind these forces. We want to discover why men in these markets act in the way they do.

3   'Every sane person understands that individuals do not emerge from the womb with preferences ready made and would like to understand preference formation. Everyone agrees that the modelling of institutions by neoclassical economics is too sparse. No one considers that we have a satisfactory account of expectation formations. No one believes that any actual economy can be studied free of initial conditions ("history")' (Hahn, 1975, p. 363).

    If so, may the time not have come to make our conceptual apparatus reflect the truth of these commonplace observations?

4   At a first glance it may seem odd, to Austrian economists in particular, that a market process may engender a restriction rather than a widening of the range of action open to some traders, quite apart from the restraints imposed by income and wealth. We have to bear in mind that merchants who believe they can spend their time more profitably than by haggling with their customers can in fact do so only if, in the time gained, they can produce something else for which the market is prepared to pay them. There never was, to be sure, a world in which traders of equal wealth faced ranges of action of exactly equal width, but the evolution of the modern market economy has no doubt made these inequalities more pronounced.

    From a wider perspective, no doubt, we have to see in our phenomenon an instance of the Process of Rationalization, the central process of Western civilization. We have to remember, though, that Max Weber insisted, in this context, on drawing the distinction between *substantive* and *formal rationality*.

5   A speculator hopes to gain from price movements over time. He can do so only by hoarding or dishoarding the objects of speculation. Accumulation or decumulation of stocks is thus a concomitant of speculation.

    Such stock movements may offset or reinforce discrepancies in the flows of supply and demand. An excess supply may be hoarded, an excess demand met from existing stock. On the other hand, however, an excess supply may be aggravated by the unloading of stock by speculators turned bearish. An excess demand may be similarly aggravated.

    What will happen in speculative markets depends in each case on the constellation of bullish and bearish expectations and the influence exercised on them by the daily flow of the news as interpreted in each market. Accordingly, as Kaldor explained in 1939, whether speculation is 'stabilizing' or 'destabilizing' depends on the circumstances of the case.

6 'In Kaleckian fashion post-Keynesian theorists divide markets into two broad categories: one, "competitive" flexprice markets in which prices are determined much in the same manner as orthodox theory tells us; and the other, "fixprice" markets in which prices reflect both "normal" production costs . . . and the demand for retained profits to finance planned investment expenditures.

The flexprice markets are mainly those concerned with the trading of raw materials and primary foodstuffs' (Kenyon, 1979, p. 34).

7 'It is held that in Keynesian economics prices are assumed to be unaffected by expansion until full employment and then *only* prices will be affected; allowance for bottlenecks modifies this proposition. The current conventional wisdom is that Keynes "nullified the Marshallian adjustment by means of prices" and proposed quantity adjustment instead. Any reader who has got this far must realise that simply is not so' (Chick, 1983, p. 271). Later on she adds that 'it is quite obvious that in the general case a rise in demand will affect *both* price and output and that the question of how much of each requires more than a mechanistic simultaneous-equation model for an intelligent reply' (ibid., p. 277).

8 Mayer, in criticizing Pareto's formulations, finds that they contain 'nichts an Darstellung des tatsächlichen Vorganges der Preisbildung, die der österreichischen Theorie das wesentliche Erkenntnisziel ist' (Mayer, 1930, p. 13).

9 For an interesting argument which reaches the same conclusion along parallel, but different, lines, see Lee (1984), esp. pp. 158–9.

10 'This axiom is the backbone of mainstream economics; it is the assumption that any good is a substitute for any other good. If the demand for good x goes up, its price will rise inducing demand to spill over to the now relatively cheaper substitute good y' (Davidson, 1984, p. 567).

7

Concluding Remarks

I

Before proceeding to examine certain conclusions that might be drawn from the line of thought set forth in previous chapters we have to warn the reader against some others, two in particular, that in our view would be unwarranted. The first of these concerns certain consequences of the indeterminate nature of economic events in a world of uncertainty for human action, and the charge of 'nihilism' often hurled at those who emphasize the ineluctable character of such indeterminateness; the second, the legitimate scope of the notion of equilibrium.

In the first place, a world of uncertainty clearly is not a world of chaos. To say that economic phenomena cannot be predicted in the sense we expect such activity from a science is not to say that men are unable to form expectations about the future outcome of the actions they presently are planning. Our inability to predict future events in no way prevents us from making forecasts about the success of our actions, forecasts which may of course be falsified by later events. Indeed, the former compels us to undertake the latter. Making such forecasts is a human, not a scientific activity.

Nor does our inability to predict mean that the economist as an observer of the social scene is prevented from describing the conduct of agents pursuing ends in an uncertain world and forming expectations in the course of such pursuit. In fact, again, it is only in the absence of mechanical causation that such description of human action in terms of means and ends is called for and makes sense.

Men make plans before they act and later on try to carry them out. Collision of the plans conceived by different agents is a daily occurrence and is of course of the essence of competition. (A competitive market process with consistency of plans constitutes a contradiction in terms. If such consistency were ever to be attained the process would come to an end.) Each plan, embodying a project of action in the future, is orientated towards a future state of affairs conceived in the form of expectations. In fitting expectations into their plans of action men of course bring their experience to bear on them, but since this activity, like the making of (ideal or real) typical models, always involves abstraction from some, and accentuation of other, elements of experience, no two men do it in the same fashion. In reality expectations almost always diverge between agents, and the same agent's expectations will vary over time under the influence of the daily stream of news. To elucidate the variegated activity men engage in in revising their expectations is one of the tasks of the economist. In accomplishing it he has to remember that, as we saw earlier, the wide variety of human minds finds a variety of intriguing expressions in a variety of markets.

The impossibility of prediction thus in no way prevents us from concerning ourselves with the formation of expectations. Indeed, as we saw, it is the very absence of mechanical causation that compels us to do so. As regards 'nihilism', this appears to be a term more appropriate to describing the mentality of those who, blind to the variegated activity of human minds when engaged in the formation of expectations, are frantically searching for links of mechanical causation where there are none, than to that of those who do their best to draw the attention of their colleagues to the problems we all face.

The other unwarranted conclusion of which we have to beware concerns legitimate and illegitimate uses of the notion of equilibrium. We must take great care in distinguishing between them. Nothing said in earlier chapters in criticism of this notion would entitle us to discard it altogether or to expunge it from the vocabulary of the economist. Equilibrium indeed has its legitimate uses, but to spell out what they are requires some effort as well as unremitting attention to the springs of human action. To our knowledge, no such effort has ever been forthcoming within the main tradition of neoclassical thought. Since the days of Walras it appears to have been simply taken for granted that a unifying principle which serves us well as a tool for the explanation of individual action (on the micro-level) will serve us equally well as a tool for the explanation of the interaction of millions of individuals in thousands of markets (on what really is a macro-level, even though this word is not usually used for this purpose). There is, however, no reason why this should be so and, indeed, some reason to doubt it. To understand this we have to turn to some fundamental problems of economics.

To act rationally means to act consistently. Experience teaches all of us that in action we cannot hope to succeed unless we learn to bring the various plans we are simultaneously pursuing into some form of consistency. Equilibrium of the individual, of household and firm, denotes a situation in which the individual has exhausted all those gains he might possibly make by removing all the inconsistencies between the various plans he is simultaneously pursuing. As such the notion of equilibrium makes very good sense. As a balance sheet, however, only has a definite meaning as long as it encompasses assets under the control of the same owner, so that the evaluation of each asset reflects acts of the same mind (usually an appointee's), but loses this meaning once we pass out of this sphere of control by a single mind (the typical problem of valuation of assets where two companies are to merge and the two sets of directors put different values on the assets of each), so the notion of equilibrium loses its clear and precise meaning once we step out of the sphere of control exercised by one individual over his acts.

Equilibrium of interaction between individuals, households and firms, i.e. between different minds, is clearly a problematic notion. A number of individuals may of course concert their actions so as to reap the gains attainable from the removal of inconsistencies between their plans (coordination of plans and efforts) but, firstly, such coordination becomes notoriously more difficult as the number of cooperators increases and informal agreement gives way to formal and enforceable contract. More important, secondly, is the fact that in a capitalistic market economy such forms of cooperative action cannot occupy a prominent place. Here competition is the dominant form of interaction between individuals and here the problematic character of interaction is clearly to be seen.

In most of the literature of neoclassical orthodoxy we look in vain for a discussion of this important problem. Nobody seems to doubt that the notion of equilibrium may legitimately be used on any level, individual or otherwise. What appears to have happened here to the notion of equilibrium is that it was, as it were, pulled up by its roots and transplanted to an alien soil. This is not to say that the problem of interaction did not make itself felt. It did, but was not recognized as what it is. It was disposed of, rather than solved, by the introduction, in his Edgeworthian or Walrasian form, of the universal auctioneer. This of course meant an attempt to solve the problem of interaction of different minds by the introduction of a fictitious single mind to which all the problems of price formation are present at the same moment. In other words, this was an attempt to dispose of a real problem by means of a purely formal device. It is, alas, characteristic of the desiccated formalism which for half a century has dominated economic thought that those who unguardedly imbibed its atmosphere soon lost their ability to distinguish between solving a problem of human action and devising a formal scheme within which it can be made to vanish from our sight. Towards the end of this chapter we shall return to the subject of the universal auctioneer.

Equilibrium has its uses. For all that has just been said, it would be quite wrong to conclude from it that all use made of the notion of equilibrium outside the sphere of action of the individual must be illegitimate. Marshall's partial equilibrium model is a striking counter-example in which interaction between producers, consumers and merchants, though on a strictly limited scale, appears to make economic sense.

We may refer to what we said about Marshall and his work in chapter 1, including note 1, but now have to look at all this from a different perspective. There we were interested in Marshall as a theorist of the market process, the intra-market process as we called it. Now, by contrast, it is Marshall the equilibrium thinker, the creator of the partial equilibrium model, who attracts our attention. We shall try to show that by introducing severe restrictions on the movement of variables in his model, by impounding, as it were, several of the more troublesome forces of interaction, Marshall, up to a point, succeeded in creating a model within the framework of which equilibrium and interaction between (a somewhat limited number of) individuals can be reconciled. It seems to us that, all things considered, we are entitled to say that Marshallian partial equilibrium analysis marks the limit to which the notion of equilibrium may be stretched and still be of some use to us. Neoclassical general equilibrium, by contrast, lies beyond this limit. How did Marshall accomplish what he did?

One of the main weaknesses of Paretian general equilibrium stems from the fact that, if this model is to be of any relevance to reality at all, the variability of the variables of our system must be restricted:

the 'data', i.e. the independent variables, must change, if at all, at considerable intervals while quantities and prices, the dependent variables, must possess high velocity of adjustment. The full implications of each change of data as regards quantities and prices must have come into view before the next change takes place. Otherwise it would be difficult to speak of 'adjustment to change'. Needless to say, in a world of specific and durable capital equipment with rapid technological progress such conditions are hard to find, in particular if, like the general equilibrium model, our system is to encompass the whole world.

In Marshall's partial equilibrium world, by contrast, we are living in a restricted environment as regards time and space. The repercussions of most of the changes occurring elsewhere in the world never reach our valley. So with us changes of data are indeed few and far between. The problems of adjusting quantities of goods produced to changes in demand are ruled out and referred to the 'long period'. In the short period such changes in demand affect prices only. Prices, on the other hand, are fully flexible and in the short run have to bear the whole burden of adjustment to change. They are set by merchants who try to maximize their turnover and whose minds are attuned to market opportunities. While each one of them need not be aware of more than one or a few opportunities it is an essential property of our short period that no opportunity arising within it remains unexploited and that a uniform market price emerges at the end of it.

Speculation, on the other hand, in the sense of buying in one period in order to sell in the future, cannot exist and is ruled out. Merchants keep such stocks as will enable them to even out sudden fluctuations in demand and supply within our period. They give no thought to what may happen in the next period, or, if they do, such thought does not affect any outcome germane to our model. In other words, the merchant acts as an arbitrageur on a limited scale, and where he carries stocks he engages in intertemporal transactions for a limited period. He is a man who, sharp-eyed but with limited horizon, operates within a limited area. It is the existence of all these limitations that in partial equilibrium, a human world without artificial 'constraints', makes a determinate outcome plausible to us.

II

We are pleading for what in chapter 5 we called a *thrust towards subjectivism* in the central area of economic theory. In previous chapters we have elucidated our case with regard to the various areas of micro and macroeconomics which might be affected by it, but we have not as yet had occasion to look at it from the perspective of the history of economic thought. It is true that throughout this book we often have, as one should, discussed present problems of economic theory in historical perspective; how else could we hope fully to understand them? But we have not as yet made an attempt to see the present case for a thrust towards subjectivism using the history of thought as our perspective.

In going about this task we face a number of difficulties two of which at least have to be mentioned. Firstly, subjectivism in economic thought has a relatively short history. Its start is usually dated to the 'subjective revolution' of the 1870s. Secondly, in all disciplines history of thought is as a rule written from the perspective of the dominant orthodoxy, a position economic subjectivism has never yet achieved. In the most notable contribution to the historiography of economic thought in this century, Schumpeter's *History of Economic Analysis* (1954) the author, though well acquainted with subjectivism as he grew up in the Austrian school in the first decade of this century, pointedly ignores the achievements of Austrian subjectivism. The fervour of his adherence to the creed of positivism rendered him unable to do justice to his teachers.

We might once more quote what Professor Hayek wrote more than 40 years ago: 'And it is probably no exaggeration to say that every important advance in economic theory during the last hundred years was a further step in the consistent application of subjectivism' (1955, p. 31), but this statement, true as it is, will probably appeal only to those who already have an attitude somewhat sympathetic towards subjectivism.

In what follows we shall attempt to substantiate Professor Hayek's statement by showing that subjectivism's two great achievements to date, utility and expectations, have both caused what might be called a 'shift of paradigm', in the sense that no sooner had these ideas been absorbed by a majority of economists than it became quite impossible for these to continue to look at certain matters in the same way as they had done before. Subjective utility and divergent expectations have both profoundly affected the nature of economic thought.

As regards the former, this is most readily seen if we follow Sir John Hicks in regarding the 'subjective revolution' of the 1870s as not just the replacement of one theory of value by another, but as a real shift of paradigm when economic science turned from *plutology* to *catallactics* (as quoted above in chapter 2, p. 25).

Classical economics was, at least originally, a pragmatic discipline. Its aim was to study means to increase the 'wealth of nations', its orientation thus to a macroeconomic magnitude. It needed a measure of wealth, and the classical notion of value was primarily designed to serve this need. Production and distribution of wealth was what really mattered. The consumer was an outsider, not an economic agent. If anything, he destroyed what was potential wealth. As long as economics was plutology, the science of wealth, there was no place for him in it. Markets, in classical doctrine, contained producers and merchants only. All this changed when subjective utility replaced objective (and measurable) cost of production as the source of value.

Economics now had to find a place for the consumer. It was he, after all, who now bestowed value on objects. All non-consumer goods were now shown to have at best purely derivative value. Moreover, it was of the very nature of the new dispensation that, not consumers as a social class, but each consumer as an individual would now assign value to objects which become economic goods solely as a result of his action. The despised outsider not only became an economic agent, he at once moved to the centre of the stage.

Economics as a discipline, however, could no longer retain its macroeconomic orientation since it had lost its measure of wealth. Almost imperceptibly to contemporaries, a major shift of paradigm took place. Classical plutology turned into catallactics, a science of markets, in which relations between buyers and sellers in a network of markets became the centre of attention and prices formed in these markets the new object of study. Merchants now functioned as inter-mediaries between producers and consumers in these markets. As Hicks wrote,

> it was becoming easier to think of 'individuals' having given wants, or given utility functions, than to swallow the homogeneous 'wealth' of the Old Political Economy. It was easier to think of the economic system as a system of interrelated markets (Walras) or as an adjustment of means to ends (Menger) than to keep up the fiction of the social product any longer (Hicks, 1976, p. 214).

It also was becoming easier, we should have thought, to see the *catallaxis*, the new world of linked markets, as a natural stage for the display of acts of the human mind in all its manifold variety, grasping and applying ever new knowledge that all too soon becomes obsolete. Whilst, by contrast, 'given utility functions' appear to belong to a very different world, namely a world of formalism, a realm of reaction to circumstances rather than of active minds. The reason why given utility functions make but little sense is that the human mind never stands still.

In turning to the introduction of expectations into the central area of economic theory in the 1920s and 1930s as our second instance of a successful 'thrust towards subjectivism' we encounter even more difficulties than in the case of subjective utility. In facing them it is all the more necessary for us to bear in mind throughout that in the real world expectations mean divergent expectations, both between individuals and over time for the same individual.

Our difficulties here stem from various sources. In the first place, while the origin of subjective utility in economic theory is readily traced to the works of Jevons, Menger and Walras all appearing within a few years of one another, this is not so with regard to expectations.

While, as we pointed out in chapter 5, it is convenient and justifiable to date the emergence of expectations in Anglo-Saxon economics to chapter 15 in Keynes' *Treatise*, the contribution made by Wicksell's pupils (Lindahl, Myrdal, Lundberg) must not be forgotten. Nor should we overlook the fact, emphasized by Professor Kregel, that in English economics of the 1920s the importance of expectations was appreciated. As he says, 'This may be due to the fact that, unlike the European tradition, English neoclassicism was more concerned with the analysis of actual markets and market institutions' (Kregel, 1977, p. 496). We also have to remember that in all applied economics, whenever speculation came up for discussion, the subject of expectations could hardly be avoided. For all this, the fact remains that before the 1930s divergent expectations were not widely regarded as having a place in the terminology of economic theory.

Our second difficulty arises from the fact that the emergence of expectations as a theoretical notion is bound up with the 'Keynesian revolution'. It is hardly an exaggeration to say that without expectations as a source of important economic forces, the Keynesian revolution could not have taken place in the form it did (which is not to say of course that it would not or could not have taken place at all without them). On the other hand, Keynes, as we explained in chapter 5, treated expectations in a somewhat haphazard fashion, for example in the theory of the multiplier they have no part at all. There is even something to be said for the belief that it was only when, in reply to critics and doubters, Keynes came to write his famous article in the *Quarterly Journal of Economics*, February 1937, that he fully perceived the significance of divergent and volatile expectations for what he had to say. It can hardly surprise us in these circumstances that, at the time, most economists, bewildered as they were by the Keynesian revolution and confused by some of its manifestations, failed entirely to perceive the thrust towards subjectivism as one of the major forces impelling it. After all, it took Professor Shackle's sustained and undaunted efforts over several decades to bring it home to us.

We find a good test of the occurrence of a major shift of paradigm in the shift of perspective from which successive generations of observers view identical problems. Today no economist, whatever his affiliations, would be able to look at problems concerning the magnitude and direction of investment without taking account of expectations, but in the 1920s the majority of economists did. Nobody today can any longer take it for granted, as economists did around 1930, that owing to the *modus operandi* of the capital market all planned savings will be invested. Expectations have become an essential part of our perspective.

This emphasis on expectations constitutes an achievement of subjectivism. Unfortunately it is even today not generally acknowledged as such. Opponents of subjectivism, for reasons we can understand, have made attempts to defuse expectations by trying to obscure their meaning as acts of various minds. 'Rational expectations', a notion which of late has become fashionable in some quarters, are essentially an attempt to emasculate expectations on the part of those who, while they cannot deny their practical significance in a world of uncertainty, are fearful of the consequences of a wider and deeper understanding of what they really mean for the stability of their doctrinal edifice. Divergent and volatile expectations of course are neither rational nor irrational, they are a fact of economic life.

We are pleading for another thrust towards subjectivism by way of the introduction of the notion of the market as a process into the central area of economic theory. We believe that this notion would provide us with the means for a deeper understanding of the ways in which a market economy functions, for instance, by enabling us to appreciate the kaleidic nature of the network of plans that underlies all action. It seems obvious that no such understanding can be attained as long as we assume from the start that all these plans are, or can readily be made, consistent. We believe that the notion of the market as a process would be a useful tool for describing the outcome of a constellation of inconsistent plans. But what else would then happen to the perspective of economists, for what other types of work our tool might prove useful, we do not and cannot know. The perspectives that will be adopted by generations yet to come remain as unknowable as future interest rates are in our world, and points of view, perspectives, and even conceptual schemes are, alas, as fugitive as the years.

III

We must now turn to the relations between economics and history. The subject has been with us for a long time. Obscured for a while by the arid formalism that has dominated economic thought for half a century, it was bound to come to the fore again as soon as the high tide of formalism began to recede. We now have to take it up in order to compare some of our conclusions with points which have arisen in recent discussions on methodology.

In 1983, in his Lindau Lecture, Sir John Hicks concluded (as he had done earlier in 'Causality in Economics') 'that economics is on the edge of science and on the edge of history' (Hicks, 1984). In the earlier statement he had also said of economics that 'facing both ways, it is in a key position. So a consideration of economics, in the way we shall be considering it, may throw light in both directions' (Hicks, 1979, p. 4).

Sir John's views seem in broad conformity with the general tenor of this book and in particular with the methodological position taken up in chapter 2. If so, a couple of problems arising from such convergence have to be considered, or reconsidered.

In the first place, it seems to follow that economics, since it is in a unique key position, needs a methodology *sui generis*, one that enables economists to 'face both ways'. This would not preclude other social sciences with similar needs (politics? sociology?) from adopting it subsequently. At the moment, however, no such 'bifocal' methodology is in existence. The task of creating one rests on the shoulders of economists. We must doubt whether the majority of the present generation of economists would find it a congenial task. Few of them are well equipped to tackle it.

Looked at from another angle, however, the outlook is distinctly more hopeful. In fact, in some respect the outlook for a thrust towards the methodological autonomy of economics is brighter today than it was thirty years ago. Then, in the name of a stern philosophy of science, economists were told what they must and must not do if they were to aspire to the achievements of a 'distinct positive science'. Today such positivism is in disarray. Few philosophers of science today would presume to lay down general rules of procedure which all those pursuing knowledge anywhere must follow. Philosophy of science is no longer a prescriptivist discipline. The aim of its research today is to find whatever has promoted and is likely to promote the 'growth of knowledge'. In the much more relaxed atmosphere prevailing today the right of economists to choose methods which suit their own purposes, though not perhaps in accordance with the canon of a doctrine of positivism laying claim to universal validity, can hardly be challenged. The way to a bifocal method such as Hicks's diagnosis of the position of economics entails seems open.

This, to be sure, is not the first time the role of economics as a discipline cognate to history is coming under discussion. A century ago, in Britain and Germany, a number of distinguished scholars launched a bitter attack on classical economics. The main ground of their attack was that classical doctrine was unhistorical, that (so they said) it had no place for institutions and the state, for policy or morality. Their views were of course vigorously disputed by the leading economic theorists of the day. Carl Menger and the Austrians of the first generation distinguished themselves by upholding economic theory, but it was less clear that they were actually defending the classical position, the primary objective of the attack.

The *Methodenstreit* ended in the first decade of this century in an atmosphere of weariness. As often happens with learned disputes, it petered out rather than ended with a victory for one side when both of them had exhausted their stock of ammunition. By more or less general consent the inconclusive outcome found its expression in a mode of coexistence: the analytical and the historical method were each to be regarded as legitimate approaches to economic life. No doubt this *modus vivendi* suited the neo-Kantian spirit of the times (the early years of this century) in that the same object of experience (economic phenomena) yielded two different objects of knowledge depending on the angle (method) from which they were viewed.

A mode of coexistence having thus been established, a dignified silence fell upon our area which lasted several decades. But the strength of the Historical School of economics had been sapped. When formalism in economic theory won its triumph around 1930 this school had virtually ceased to exist.

Once we adopt the new Hicksian perspective, however, the old problem of the relationship between economics and history emerges in a new guise. What is at issue now is no longer a mode of coexistence but terms of cooperation. If economics is 'on the edge of history' economists, or at least those in charge of this part of their building, will have to seek the cooperation of historians. On what terms? There can be no question of economists turning themselves into narrative historians or historians having to become economists. But might there not be other forms of writing and studying history more amenable to the embrace of economic theory? We also have to realize, as one of the implications of the Hicksian view, that we must see the present as the outcome of history, and present economic problems accordingly. If so, current economic events can hardly be regarded as recurrent phenomena of an immutable nature.

Fortunately we are well equipped to confront this encounter of economics and history. We may refer to what was said on this subject in chapter 2, in particular in section III. We may even reiterate here:

> The simplest way to describe the relationship between the analytical social sciences (praxeology) and the various kinds of history is in terms of the respective parts they play with regard to the production and use of ideal-typical conceptual schemes. Briefly, the former produce and the latter use them. They are used, as it were, as a foil against which to hold 'real events' so as to bring out particular properties of the latter by comparison. In particular, such conceptual schemes permit historians to classify 'events' in terms of the latter's proximity or distance from them (above, p. 34).

A number of formidable difficulties nevertheless stand in the way of this cooperation. In the first place, economists as suppliers of models, like all suppliers, must study the needs of their customers, the historians, and take their orientation from their market, while the canon of fashion appears to dictate that model-building is to be regarded as an exercise of *l'art pour l'art*. Few, if any, economists seem ready today for, if capable of, practising this aspect of cooperation.[1]

A more intricate problem concerns the definition of the terms of cooperation. In the production of models, is it possible to lay down general rules about the level of abstraction to be aimed at? We often are told that economic theory is concerned with 'recurrent patterns of events', but not with all events. The level of abstraction to be aimed at in economic theory thus would appear to be geared to such forms of recurrence, while it is for the historian to 'fill in the details' in applying theories to concrete events. Experience unfortunately teaches us that such a division of phenomena into recurrent and unique, general and particular, generic and individual, is often impossible. Even where it is possible, some recurrent phenomena may be complementary to non-recurrent ones. Also, only too often it will happen that a phenomenon recurs a number of times, but then ceases, while new ones make their entry.

It may be thought that the problems we have encountered are essentially such as are engendered by the well-known category *cetera non paria* and have to be treated accordingly, but this is not strictly so, even though some affinity exists. If it were possible, in the investigation of each event the causes of which we seek to establish, to classify all possibly relevant phenomena into those germane and those not germane to it, there would be no need at all for a qualifying clause of the indefinite character of the *ceteris paribus* clause. By contrast, such need arises where this form of classification is impossible. Here our clause permits us to establish empirical generalizations without having to engage in the irksome task of classifying phenomena that defy such classification.

The problems of cooperation may assume a new character as number of facts and length of period of time studied vary. As regards the latter, if the facts the historian studies extend over a long stretch of time, he may have to employ different theoretical models for different periods. As Hicks said at the end of his Lindau lecture, 'but the aspects of economic life which we need to select in order to make useful theories can be different at different times' (Hicks, 1984, p. 218). While it is for the historian to choose appropriate theories for the various periods he studies, it is for the economist to supply him with a sufficient variety of them.

When the historian faces large numbers of facts he may have to make a 'representative selection' in order to reduce his material to manageable size. One way to do this, as we indicated in section III of chapter 2, is to construct 'real types'. As we said there, 'Here our ideal types, have to be compared directly with the real types, and thus only indirectly with the masses of events for which the real types, as it were, stand proxy. There can be no rules for the construction of either real or ideal types, except that they must "fit together"'.

Our two instruments of thought, theoretical (ideal) and historical (real) type, will contribute most to the growth of our knowledge when they cast light upon one another and the circumstances (events) surrounding them. To this end they have to display dissimilarities as well as similarities. Without the latter we cannot compare them whilst without the former we could learn little from the comparison. To learn most we have to place our two instruments at such distance that they can best illuminate one another as well as the surrounding landscape.

Successful prediction, congruence of theory and fact, is thus for us not the highest achievement imaginable, as it would mean that the growth of our knowledge has, at least for the time being, reached its end. (Similarly as a state of perfect competition would mean the end of the competitive market process.)

Falsification of a hypothesis opens the door to its improvement. Dissimilarity between theory and historical observation, between our ideal and real type, draws our attention to problems as yet unsolved and contributes to the growth of our knowledge by widening our horizon.

In conclusion, we shall attempt to illustrate the methodological view just set forth by three examples, two of which involve theoretical concepts we have come across in earlier chapters, while the third concerns an episode in the history of thought in which an economist and a historian, both eminent men in their disciplines, signally failed to understand each other and thus were unable to come to terms that might have permitted cooperation.

In our first two examples we shall adopt what we now may call a 'Growth of Knowledge' approach, not because in current philosophy of science this happens to be the fashion of the day (in our age fashionable ideas have notoriously short lives), but because we hope that the adoption of such an approach will enable us to exhibit the mode of elucidation through confrontation between theoretical models and real types, and to show how, by the interpretation of differences at first unsuspected, but then illuminated from various perspectives, it contributes to the widening of our horizon and the growth of our knowledge. Mere falsification as such, by contrast, does not point beyond itself and yields no such benefits.

Our first example concerns the quantity theory as a theoretical model. We dealt with it at some length in chapter 5 and refer to what we said there. Nothing is easier than to falsify it, but little is to be gained by it unless we are prepared to make a comparative study of such cases, relating different events to our ideal type in a mode of confrontation. This theory was originally an empirical generalization about the relationship between quantity of money and price level. What were the *cetera* that had to remain *paria* to lend it validity? In 1911, Fisher's Quantity equation, a truism and not an empirical generalization, provided the answer. Further progress was made largely by questioning, on the basis of experience, present and historical, the constancy of magnitudes figuring as constants in this and similar other equations. It had, for instance, always been known that money has several functions. In the *Treatise* Keynes accordingly suggested dividing M, the total stock of money, into financial and industrial circulation.

The relationship between money and money substitutes by now has a fairly long history. We have to remind ourselves that when, at an early stage, the Banking School presented its argument that bank deposits are no less means of payment than bank notes are, this was a generalization that at the time was drawn from, and confined to, the English money market, and outside it did not have much validity. To that extent, at that time, the bank deposit as a means of payment was a real type. Since then things have changed. The notion of money substitute as we use it today is an abstract type. But it could not do for us what it does if it were not the product of a chain of thought that started with its earlier antecedents.

The growth of money substitutes has now reached a stage where nobody is able to say any longer what is the observable counterpart of the M of the quantity theory. Is it to be M1, M2, M3, . . . or what? The quantity theory has not so much been falsified as that we no longer know by what criterion it is to be tested. It has become inapplicable to our world. It is with a wry smile that some of us remember the days when, before the rise of econometrics, doubts about our ability to measure many economic magnitudes used to be met by the observation that there was one indubitably measurable: money!

Our second example concerns the role of intermediary agents in markets. In our view, there can be few areas of study offering more fertile ground for cooperation between economists and historians, while the prevailing climate of formalism in economic theory has rendered such cooperation difficult. We refer to what we said about markets and market processes in earlier chapters, and, in particular, to our elucidation of the role of the Marshallian merchant above.

Edgeworthian recontract and Walrasian *tâtonnement* have a place for one intermediary agent only, the universal auctioneer, a figure of grotesque pretensions. A more modern version of general equilibrium theory offers us an alternative in the form of a universal system of futures markets, one for each good and each future period, an idea hardly less absurd. But intermediary agents, auctioneers among them, exist in real markets. How should we conceptualize them?

Here we once more encounter the Marshallian merchant who seems to meet some of our needs. The circumstance that he is endowed with a limited horizon, as we saw, and operates in a limited area, is to us, however, a virtue rather than a shortcoming. For it forcibly directs our attention to the fact, congenial to our general view of markets, that merchants are not evenly spread across the world and the network of intermediation not equally closely knit in all markets.

It is only one step to our next question, whether there may not be markets in which intermediation is carried out by agents other than merchants. It will now perhaps be clear that one reason, *inter alia*, prompting us, in chapter 6, to introduce the distinction between merchants' and salesmen's markets was the desire for a tool to handle merchantless markets. We regard these two market types as real types, drawn from historical reality and hope they will shed some light on the fixprice-flexprice problem area filled with ideal types belonging to theory. We hope to learn from their confrontation.

We now turn to our third example. In Britain, in 1922, the *Methodenstreit* flared up in a new guise. It took the form of the 'empty boxes' controversy between Clapham, an economic historian, and Pigou, Marshall's successor in the Chair of Economics at Cambridge.

Clapham complained that the Marshallian concept of industries operating under diminishing or increasing returns was useless to the historian as these notions might at best be applied to production processes for concrete goods, but hardly to whole industries. He added 'that we do not, for instance, at this moment *know* under what conditions of returns coal or boots are being produced' (Clapham, 1922, p. 312).

Pigou, in his angry reply, accused his opponent of misunderstanding the nature of economic theory.

> Dr Clapham appears to hold that, provided as boxes they cannot be filled, it is self-evident they can serve no useful purpose of this kind. In that I venture to suggest that he is mistaken, that he has, in fact, misunderstood altogether the nature of the work he is belittling . . .
> To take the categories of increasing and diminishing returns out of their

setting and to speak of them as though they were a thing that could be swept away without injury to the whole *corpus* of economics is a very perverse proceeding (Pigou, 1922, pp. 460–1).

From our standpoint, what matters most is that Pigou here virtually denies any obligation economists may have towards historians. This denial is stated fairly explicitly when he says, 'Even a thoroughly realistic economic science would not, in and for itself, make any great appeal to me. Practical usefulness, not necessarily of course immediate and direct, but still practical usefulness of some sort is what I look for from this particular department of knowledge' (ibid., p. 461).

So our two protagonists were unable to find terms of cooperation and no growth of knowledge resulted from their encounter.

It is sometimes suggested that the remarkable progress of economics in the Years of High Theory (1926–39) constituted entirely an endogenous development of thought and owed little to confrontation of theory and reality. 'The demonstration by Piero Sraffa that there were logical inconsistencies in the laws of returns had more effect than the applied economists' complaints of unrealism in stimulating the search for new models based on the assumption of imperfect competition' (Deane, 1983, p. 10).

We must remember, however, that however high the level of abstraction in Sraffa's critique, at a decisive point in his argument he based it on an appeal to the reality of modern industry and the prevalence of increasing returns in the equilibrium position of the firm.

> Everyday experience shows that a very large number of undertakings – and the majority of those which produce manufactured consumers' goods – work under conditions of individual diminishing costs . . .
>
> . . . Business men, who regard themselves as being subject to competitive conditions, would consider absurd the assertion that the limit to their production is to be found in the internal conditions of production in their firm, which do not permit of the production of a greater quantity without an increase in cost . . . This method of regarding the matter appears the most natural, and that which adheres to the reality of things (Sraffa, 1926, p. 543).

As a theorist, thus, Sraffa did not share at all Pigou's aversion to realism in economic theory, but did not hesitate to make use of it as an argument. The 'business men' in the above quotation are, in our terminology, a 'real type' drawn from modern industry. Sraffa explicitly contrasts their views with the concepts (ideal types) of the Marshallian theory of costs which they dismiss as 'absurd'. The subsequent evolution of the theories of imperfect and monopolistic competition in the wake of the discussions engendered by Sraffa's onslaught on the Marshallian heritage conformed to the same pattern, even though they remained somewhat unsatisfactory at first in depicting competitive markets as 'states of affairs', that is, modes of static equilibrium, instead of as dynamic processes. Nevertheless, growth of knowledge took place, set in motion by the encounter of theory and reality.

In this book we have made an attempt to understand the nature of events in a market economy and to trace the forces impelling market processes, whether convergent or divergent, to the springs of human action, that is, our acts of will and imagination, as well as those acts which grasp experience and turn it into knowledge.

In chapter 1 an outline of a scheme of our comprehension of market processes was sketched. In subsequent chapters we elucidated some aspects of them from a variety of points of view. We pleaded for a further thrust towards subjectivism, after utility and expectations, in the hope that a theory of the market process, along these lines, will be able to make contributions to the growth of knowledge. In the end we reached the conclusion that, if economics is a discipline on the edge of history no less than the edge of science, the methods pursued in it will have to take account of this fact.

NOTES

1 This is not to say that such a change of attitude is impossible, or that, while possible, it will not happen. It is, rather, to say that it can only happen as part and parcel of a wider process of general reorientation which would inevitably be slow. One of the main obstacles to such a course probably lies in the present attitude of the scribes and publishers of the textbook industry, who, taking their orientation from a mass market, can give but scant attention to the subtlety of methodological thought.

Appendix

The Market is not a Clockwork

For about twelve years economic theory, the central area of the economic sciences, has been in a noticeable state of crisis. According to an opinion widespread among both economists and noneconomists, the causes of this crisis have to be sought mainly in the unfavourable and often tempestuous circumstances of the times, such as the ubiquitous and seemingly irresistible inflation which around 1970 turned into 'stagflation', and the circumstances concomitant to the collapse of the Bretton Woods system, all of which economic theory has to account for. Partly this explanation certainly holds true. Economic theory could never help taking its orientation from the events of its time and its world, and drawing inspiration from them. It was in the years of inflation accompanying the war against Napoleon and of the Continental blockade that the young Ricardo first gained fame. The present-day controversy between Keynesians and Monetarists turns on the question of how best to master the inflation of our times.

However, this purely historical interpretation, no matter how justified it might be in detail, does not go to the root of today's crisis and fails to do justice to its depth. It offers a fundamentally inadequate characterization of the present state of affairs in economic theory. For in the background of the scene a crisis of the method of economic thinking is taking shape. The question arises, to what extent the style of economic thought which has been predominant for about half a century, at least in the Western world, can do justice to the problems of human action in a rapidly changing world, and, in particular, in a tempestuous epoch. To understand the relevance of this question with all its implications demands an explanation drawn from the history of ideas.

Today's crisis in economic theory is, above all, a crisis of that uniform style of economic thinking which triumphed about half a century ago in a form which was given to it by Pareto and was borrowed from classical mechanics. Before 1930 this style did not prevail as a general method of thought. To be sure, it already had outstanding advocates such as Edgeworth in England and Fisher in America, but, both within and outside the Anglo-Saxon world, there existed a number of schools of economic theory inspired by other styles of thought. In the history of economic thought epochs of convergence, such as that of the predominance of the Classical School before 1870, alternate with those of divergence, such as that between 1870 and 1930.

While up to about 1920 most economists considered discovering 'economic laws' the major task of their science, they did so without thereby wishing to incur any major methodological commitments. In the *Methodenstreit* both, Menger and Schmoller, the leaders of the two opposing schools, argued in terms of the quest for laws, while admittedly meaning quite different things by this notion. The idea of trying to expand determinism, then thought resident solely in the realm of laws, to the entire network of exchange relations within an economy did not occur to anybody who did not belong to the Lausanne School.

Only some years after Pareto's death in 1923, did determinism in the form of general equilibrium theory and with the conscious link to classical mechanics begin its victorious advance in the Western world. To be sure, the interdependence of all markets as a characteristic feature of a market economy had been quite an important concern in classical economics, which found expression in the equality of profit rates, but to classical economists this interdependence did not yet entail the interdependence of *all* prices and quantities. Now, however, it came to be believed that the skeleton of all truth was to be found in just this interdependence. The determinism of all quantities and prices was proclaimed.

It was hardly an accident that the events described took place in the era of the rise of logical positivism. The answers to the questions of what warranted the connection between the different floors of this impressive edifice of science, as well as that between the system as a whole and economic reality, were to be found in the fact that the measurability of the equilibrium data would guarantee their verifiability, and the possibility of making concrete predictions about quantities and prices would ensure their falsifiability. This rendered it necessary to create a new body of measurable concepts and a technique for measuring economic variables. This need, in its turn, duly gave rise to a new branch of economic science, econometrics. In 1931 the International Econometric Society was founded, an event welcomed by Schumpeter as a landmark of progress.

This deterministic method of thought reveals its debt to classical mechanics most prominently in the fact that here economic action is not regarded as, first, being conceived in the mind, then translated into plans, and finally implemented in reality. The human actor here appears as entangled in the interplay of two polar forces, the incentive to utility maximization and the impediments resulting from the scarcity of commodities and means of production. Action is not the issue here, but reaction to given circumstances. This form of thought is incompatible with voluntarism.

The name that has since become established for this is 'the neo-classical paradigm'. In our view it would be more appropriate to speak here of *late classical formalism*. To be sure, the doctrines of classical economics were not altogether alien to a sometimes rather 'robust' mechanical style of thinking (law of uniformity of the rate of profits). They regarded 'natural price', determined by costs of production, as, so to speak, the centre of gravity of each market. To no classical economist, however, would it have occurred to consider each market price and each quantity exchanged in a market as being determined by identifiable market forces. The neoclassical paradigm, in part, rests on an astonishing lack of ability on the part of many of its adherents to realize the limits of determinism as a form of economic thought.

The success of the 'Keynesian Revolution' after 1936 at first left the hegemony of the late classical formalism, that had just gained its ascendancy in the 1930s, unchanged, especially since the *General Theory of Employment* was presented in the form of a short-run equilibrium model. The relationships between macroeconomic aggregates, such as the level of employment, consumption, investment etc. representing, at first glance, Keynes's main concern, actually seemed to call for econometric measurement. Without any evident difficulty Keynesian theory in the 1940s became incorporated into the paradigm of late classical formalism under the name of *neoclassical synthesis*.

Some of Keynes's friends and students in Cambridge protested in vain that 'this was not what the master had meant'. For the time being their voices found no echo.

Nevertheless, Keynes's relationship to econometrics was always problematical. A rather trenchant critique of the work of the econometrician Tinbergen in which he altogether questioned the possibility of 'quantitative' economic theory was published in 1939/40, the first year of the war, but did not attract much attention. Moreover, Keynes was a pragmatist. Whatever, as a social thinker, he might have thought of the econometricians, Keynes, the British economic strategist of the Second World War, could certainly not dispense with their help. The controversy with Tinbergen was soon forgotten.

Today we know more, especially thanks to the publication of his correspondence as part of the *Collected Writings* of Keynes. In a letter to Harrod dated 16 July 1938 Keynes strongly emphasizes that economic science is a *moral science*. The method of the natural sciences is not applicable. This characteristic passage then follows:

> It is as though the fall of the apple to the ground depended on the apple's motives, on whether it is worthwhile falling to the ground, and whether the ground wanted the apple to fall, and on mistaken calculations on the part of the apple as to how far it was from the centre of the earth (*Collected Writings*, vol. XIV, p. 300).

Here we encounter Keynes as a subjectivist to whom the key to understanding economic action lies in the aim-choosing and purpose-pursuing acts of the human mind.

Since the publication of the *General Theory* in 1936 the discussion of Keynes has never actually ceased. It would hardly be an exaggeration to say that today every economic theorist with a reputation to lose holds his own view on 'what Keynes really meant'.

As to our topic, it is an important fact that only fairly late, actually only during the 1960s, the insight slowly gained ground that, on the one hand, many difficulties in the interpretation of Keynes's thought within the framework of the late classical formalism ultimately stem from an incompatibility of styles of thought, and that, on the other hand, in the Keynesian system of thought itself there inheres a strange contradiction between form and content. For Keynes, the real aim of his theory was actually the *understanding* ('*Verstehen*' in Max Weber's sense) of human action in a given institutional situation. In odd contrast to that, however, he to a large extent made use of a conceptual apparatus which was marked by formalism. No wonder this incongruous mixture of styles caused some severe misunderstandings.

It is the merit of George Shackle, who is apparently almost unknown in Germany, to have first pointed out this strange contradiction. He discovered a deep contradiction between the method and the meaning of Keynes's book. While his method is of the type of general equilibrium analysis, that is to say, the interpretation of human action as reaction to given circumstances, his true meaning is that just such rationality, owing to the nature of things, is often impossible as men confront an unknown and unknowable future.

After some initial hesitation (as Shackle can hardly be counted one of them), the Cambridge School adopted this interpretation of Keynes's work as an expression of the 'interpretative' method of thought. Outside Cambridge also it is gaining more and more adherents nowadays.

Briefly, we have to deal here with the fact that the unknown future and the irrevocable past bear fundamentally different importance for human action. This fact has important consequences. On the one hand, it follows that a mathematical notion of time, naturally having to abstract from these differences, cannot do justice to the problems of economic action. On the other hand, it follows that at any point in time men act according to their expectations which are individually different and do change over time. The amount of current investment does not depend upon the profitability of investment in the past, but upon today's expectations of future profits. The market economy has enabled Stock Exchanges and forward markets to evolve, markets in which transactions are orientated towards the future. Without the divergence of individual expectations there would be no transactions in these markets. Without changes of expectations fed by the flow of daily news the daily price fluctuations so characteristic of these markets could hardly exist.

Keynes certainly did not introduce expectations into economic theory: Wicksell's Swedish students (Lindahl, Myrdal) did that in the late 1920s. Nor can it be denied that occasionally he dealt with expectations quite arbitrarily, not to say violently. He introduced them into his theory whenever he needed them and ignored them whenever he did not. Nevertheless, it remains a fact that by his emphasis on the role of expectations in important market processes he promoted the cause of the hermeneutic mode of thought in economic theory.

Since about the mid-1960s a decline of late classical formalism is to be observed. There are a number of causes which, in tempestuous season, have brought this about.

The late classical general equilibrium model requires a stationary world. Once we allow for change in the data serious problems arrive. When data change faster than quantities of goods and prices can adjust an equilibrium might not be achievable. This was demonstrated by Kaldor 50 years ago. Only as long as we deal with few and infrequent changes of data and high speeds of adjustment in the rest of the system may these difficulties be neglected.

This necessarily stationary character of the general equilibrium model became patent as soon as economists tried to apply it to economic progress, thus a non-stationary economy, and started speaking of 'steady growth'. The idea certainly is not new at all and goes back to Cassel who, almost 70 years ago, spoke of an 'evenly progressive economy' ('gleichmässig fortschreitende Wirtschaft') in his *Theoretische Sozialökonomie* (Leipzig, 1918). But experience has taught us that with growing incomes incremental income is not spent in the same proportions as income was before, that possibly totally new categories of goods will appear, and that the immobility of durable capital goods stands in the way of rapid adaptation to such changes. This shows how little room there is in reality for such constructions.

Furthermore, the discussion showed that money and credit do not fit at all into the general equilibrium model, which requires a pure barter economy.

Finally, we have to remember that in this model the mode of the distribution of wealth is a datum. Continuous capital gains and losses are incompatible with it. But in a world, such as our own, in which at any hour a stock market (or real estate market) is open somewhere such gains and losses are an hourly event. Again, the model does not fit into our world.

After all that it is hardly surprising that today we can scarcely speak of the predominance of late classical formalism any more. We note that some of the leading thinkers of this school, like Arrow in America and Hahn in Britain, are well aware of the weaknesses of their model and of their own precarious situation. Among their followers, however, this insight has not as yet gained much ground. In Chicago, it seems, one lives as within a citadel and refuses to take notice of it all. Just as with the decline of a culture we often find that its values are still maintained for many decades by the faithful masses when the cultural avantgarde has long ago turned its back on them, we find the heirs of the late classical way of thought today in a similar situation.

Into the gap created by the events mentioned there have of late moved a number of rival schools. They have appeared on the plane to announce their programmes and are now vying with each other for support. Indeed, the crisis in economic theory today finds its main outward expression in this contest between the schools. It is unlikely that one of them will gain predominance in the foreseeable future and, for the same reason as that why most economists prefer competition to monopoly, such an outcome would hardly be called for. Three of these schools are of particular interest to us.

The Freiburger Schule probably owed its rise to the special circumstances of postwar Germany. Attuned to economic reality, it was taken aback and estranged by the formalism of Anglo-Saxon economic theory of the 1950s. In the new situation we depicted, however, we may expect from it significant contributions in the future. Since Eucken it has directed its special attention to the institutions of the economic order. Nowadays there happily is almost unanimous consent that the institutional framework of economic action, of the importance of which the Scottish classics were well aware, has been unduly neglected by the formalism of the last decades. In America a Property Rights School has lately come into existence, stressing the economic significance of the institutional order. We may thus hope that the work of the Freiburger Schule will soon receive deserved appreciation also outside the German borders.

The Austrian School we find today in a promising position with some peculiar features of its own. For various reasons it was particularly exposed to the impetus of the Keynesian Revolution and suffered from it more than others. This was not changed even by the success Hayek achieved in the 1940s with his famous essays on the meaning of competition as a process and the role of social knowledge. To the Austrians, as a school and as a community, the years between 1940 and 1970 were years in the wilderness. As Hicks wrote in 1965, they were then a school 'whose voice has been almost drowned in the fanfare of the Keynesian orchestra' (Hicks, 1965, p. 185). But for about twelve years a rebirth of this school has become discernible. The decline of late classical determinism offered opportunities the Austrians could as little afford to let slip as others could.

The Austrian School has always been the school of subjectivism and methodological individualism. Its descent from the subjectivist theory of value has marked its style of thought. Naturally, its rebirth took place in the sign of subjectivism which, in the years of darkness, von Mises had espoused at New York University till very old age. The role of the human actor in the market economy was emphasized. Kirzner stressed the role of the entrepreneur neglected by the late classicism. Shackle's radical subjectivism proved congenial to this style of thought. As regards the interpretation of the market economy, one tended to view the market as a process rather than as a state of equilibrium.

Many problems remain unsolved. To rejoin disconnected threads after the return from the wilderness is one task, to weave them into a coherent pattern is another. The philosophical fundament of the school is the subject of controversy. Menger, its founder, was an Aristotelian, Mises a rationalist of the practical reason. Hayek in some of his recent writings seems to disavow rationalism in all its forms. A more perceptive regard for various nuances of the present position of the school in its relations to other schools, attuned to the opportunities offered by the current situation of economic theory in general, might also help to contribute to the solution of some of these problems.

Amidst all these occurrences the Cambridge School has distinguished itself. The bravura shown by some of its protagonists, such as the late Joan Robinson, did not remain without effect. This school, however, has always been a coalition of heterogeneous forces, and it is possible that, here as before, the defeat of the common (late classical) adversary will lead to a break-up of the alliance. We are dealing here with a coalition between the Sraffa school, whose doctrines may be classified as 'neo-Ricardianism' and which proposes the return to the classical style of thought, that is to say to the objectivism of impersonal social forces, and the Post-Keynesians who want to continue Keynes's work. But, as was shown above, Keynes was a subjectivist. It cannot surprise us that within this coalition a dispute broke out over the role of expectations the fundamental role of which the Post-Keynesians need to cling to, while to the Ricardians they are most distasteful.

It is possible to take the classical view that all economic theory has to say necessarily refers to the long run. Or we might agree with Keynes when he says that in the long run we are all dead. It is hard to see how one can hold both opinions at the same time. In this there rests the weakness of the Cambridge School.

We have described today's arena in the field of economic theory and sketched the attitudes of some of the contesting schools there. How far there will be a convergence of divergent points of view, or new disagreements, remains to be seen. That the subjectivists of different schools, that is to say, all those who view the market as a pattern of meaningful utterances of the human mind, will in the future be able to find common ground seems to us to lie distinctly within the realm of possibility.

©*Frankfurter Allgemeine Zeitung*. A German version of this paper appeared under the title 'Der Markt ist Kein Uhrwerk' in the *Frankfurter Allgemeine Zeitung*, 24 November 1984. This version translated by Cornelia Dorfschmid and revised by the author.

Bibliography

Arrow, K. (1978). The future and the present in economic life. *Economic Inquiry*, April.

Böhm-Bawerk, E. (1907). 'Capital and interest once more', *Quarterly Journal of Economics*, February.

Boland, L. A. (1978). 'Time in economics vs. economics in time: the "Hayek problem"', *Canadian Journal of Economics*, May.

Champernowne, D. G. (1972). Review of H. Theil, *Principles of Econometrics, Economic Journal*, March.

– (1973). Review of G. L. Shackle, *Epistemics and Economics, Economic Journal*, September.

Chick, V. (1981). 'Reply to Professor Harrison', *Australian Economic Papers*, December.

– (1983). *Macroeconomics after Keynes: A Reconsideration of the General Theory*. Oxford: Philip Allan.

Clapham, J. H. (1922). 'Of empty economic boxes', *Economic Journal*, September.

Davidson, P. (1978). *Money and the Real World*. London. Macmillan.

– (1984). 'Reviving Keynes's revolution', *Journal of Post Keynesian Economics*, Summer.

Deane, P. (1983). 'The scope and method of economic science', *Economic Journal*, September.

Fisher, I. (1911). *The Purchasing Power of Money*. New York: Macmillan.

Garegnani, P. (1976). 'On a change in the notion of equilibrium in recent work on value and distribution', in Murray Brown and others (eds), *Essays in Modern Capital Theory*. Amsterdam: North Holland Press.

– (1978-9). 'Notes on consumption, investment and effective demand', *Cambridge Journal of Economics*, December 1978, March 1979.

– (1979). 'A reply to Joan Robinson', *Cambridge Journal*, June.

Gordon, R. J. (ed.) (1974). *Milton Friedman's Monetary Framework. A Debate with his Critics*. Chicago. Chicago University Press.

Gram, H. and Walsh, V. C. (1983). 'Joan Robinson's economics in retrospect', *Journal of Economic Literature*, June.

Hahn, F. H. (1973). 'The winter of our discontent', *Economica*, August.

– (1975). 'Revival of political economy: the wrong issues and the wrong argument', *Economic Record*, September.

– (1977). 'Keynesian economics and equilibrium theory', in G. C. Harcourt (ed.), *The Microeconomic Foundations of Macroeconomics*. London: Macmillan.

– (1981). Review of M. Beenstock, *A Neoclassical Analysis of Macroeconomic Policy*, *Economic Journal*, December.

Hayek, F. A. (1935). 'The maintenance of capital', *Economica*, August.

– (1936). 'The mythology of capital', *Quarterly Journal of Economics*, February.

– (1937). 'Economics and knowledge', *Economica*, February.

– (1941). *The Pure Theory of Capital*. London: Routledge.

– (1949). *Individualism and Economic Order*. London: Routledge.

– (1955). *The Counter-Revolution of Science*. Glencoe: Free Press.

Hicks, J. R. (1934). 'Leon Walras', *Econometrica*.

– (1963). *The Theory of Wages*. London: Macmillan.

– (1965). *Capital and Growth*. Oxford: Clarendon Press.

– (1969). *A Theory of Economic History*. Oxford: Oxford University Press.

– (1967). *Critical Essays in Monetary Theory*. Oxford: Clarendon Press.

– (1974). 'Capital controversies: ancient and modern', *American Economic Review: Papers and Proceedings*, May.

– (1976a). 'Revolution in economics', in S. J. Latsis (ed.), *Methods and Appraisal in Economics*. Cambridge: Cambridge University Press.

– (1976b). 'Some questions of time in economics', in A. M. Tang, F. M. Westfield and J. S. Worley (eds), *Evolution, Welfare and Times in Economics: Essays in Honour of Georgescu-Roegen*. New York: Lexington Books.

– (1977). *Economic Perspectives: Further Essays on Money and Growth*. Oxford: Clarendon Press.

– (1979). *Causality in Economics*. Oxford: Blackwell.

– (1984). 'Is economics a science?', *Interdisciplinary Science Reviews*, September.

Hollis, M. and Nel, E. J. (1975). *Rational Economic Man*. Cambridge: Cambridge University Press.

Kaldor, N. (1960a). 'The determinateness of static equilibrium', in *Essays on Value and Distribution*. London: Duckworth.

– (1960b). 'Speculation and economic stability', in *Essays on Economic Stability and Growth*. London: Duckworth.

- (1960b). 'Speculation and economic stability', in *Essays on Economic Stability and Growth*. London: Duckworth.
Kenyon, P. (1979). 'Pricing', in Alfred S. Eichner (ed.), *A Guide to Post Keynesian Economics*. London: Macmillan.
Keynes, J. M. (1930). *A Treatise on Money*. 2 vols. London: Macmillan.
- (1936). *General Theory of Employment, Money and Interest*. London: Macmillan.
- (1937). 'The general theory of employment', *Quarterly Journal of Economics*, February. Reprinted in S. E. Harris (ed.), *The New Economics*. London: Dobson, 1947.
- (1973, 1979). *Collected Writings*, vols XIV (1973) and XXIX (1979). London: Macmillan.
Kirzner, I. M. (1966). *An Essay on Capital*. New York: Augustus M. Kelly.
- (1973). *Competition and Entrepreneurship*. Chicago: University of Chicago Press.
- (1976). 'The theory of capital', in E. G. Dolan (ed.), *The Foundations of Modern Austrian Economics*. Kansas City: Sheed and Ward.
- (1978). 'Economics and error', in L. M. Spadaro (ed.) *New Directions in Austrian Economics*. Kansas City: Sheed, Andrews & McMeel.
Kregel, L. A. (1976). 'Economic methodology in the face of uncertainty', *Economic Journal*, June.
- (1977). 'On the existence of expectations in English neoclassical economics', *Journal of Economic Literature*, June.
Lachmann, L. M. (1956). *Capital and its Structure*. London: Bell.
- (1977). *Capital, Expectations and the Market Process*. Kansas City: Sheed, Andrews & McMeel.
- (1978). *Capital and its Structure*. 2nd edn. Kansas City: Sheed, Andrews & McMeel.
Laidler, D. (1974). 'Information, money and the macroeconomics of inflation', *Swedish Journal of Economics*, 26–43.
Lee, F. S. (1984). 'Full cost pricing: a new wine in a new bottle', *Australian Economic Papers*, June.
Marget, A. W. (1938, 1940). *The Theory of Prices*. 2 vols. New York: Prentice-Hall.
Marshall, A. (1920). *Principles of Economics*. 8th edn. London: Macmillan.
Mayer, H. (1930). 'Die Wert- und Preisbildung der Produktionsmittel', *Economia Politica Contemporanea*, vol. II (in onore del Prof. Camillo Supino), Padua.
- (1932). 'Der Erkenntniswert der funktionellen Preistheorien', in *Wirtschaftstheorie der Gegenwart*, vol. II. Vienna: Springer.
Milgate, M. (1979). 'On the origin of the notion of "intertemporal equilibrium",' *Economica*, February.

– (1982). *Capital and Employment: A Study of Keynes's Economics*. New York: Academic Press.

Mises, L. von (1912). *Theorie des Geldes und der Umlaufsmittel*. Munich: Duncker & Humblot.

– (1943). '"Elastic expectations" and the Austrian theory of the trade cycle', *Economica*, August.

– (1949). *Human Action*. New Haven: Yale University Press.

– (1957). *Theory and History*. New Haven: Yale University Press.

– (1978). *Notes and Recollections*. New York: Libertarian Press.

Petri, F. (1978). 'The difference between long-period and short-period general equilibrium and the Capital Theory controversy', *Australian Economic Papers*, December.

Pigou, A. C. (1917). 'The value of money', *Quarterly Journal of Economics*, November.

– (1922). 'Empty boxes – a reply', *Economic Journal*, December.

– (1935). 'Net income and capital depletion', *Economic Journal*, June.

Popper, Karl R. (1957). *The Poverty of Historicism*. London: Routledge.

Richardson, G. B. (1959). 'Equilibrium, expectations and information', *Economic Journal*, June.

– (1960). *Information and Investment*. Oxford: Oxford University Press.

Robbins, Lionel (1935). *An Essay on the Nature and Significance of Economic Science*. 2nd edn. London: Macmillan.

Robinson, J. (1956). *The Accumulation of Capital*. Cambridge: Cambridge University Press.

– (1979). 'Garegnani on effective demand', *Cambridge Journal*, June, 179–80.

Rothschild, M. (1973). 'Models of market organization with imperfect information: a survey', *Journal of Political Economy*. November/December, 1283–1308.

Shackle, G. L. S. (1965). *A Scheme of Economic Theory*. Cambridge: Cambridge University Press.

– (1958). *Time in Economics*. Amsterdam: North-Holland.

– (1972a). *Epistemics and Economics*. Cambridge: Cambridge University Press.

– (1972b). 'Marginalism: the harvest', *History of Political Economy*, Fall.

Schumpeter, J. A. (1934). *The Theory of Economic Development*. Oxford, New York: Oxford University Press.

Solow, R. M. (1963). *Capital Theory and Rate of Return*. Amsterdam: North Holland.

Sraffa, Piero (1926). 'The laws of returns under competitive conditions', *Economic Journal*, December.

– (1960). *Production of Commodities by means of Commodities*. Cambridge: Cambridge University Press.

Telser, L. G. (1973). 'Searching for the lowest price', *American Economic Review: Papers and Proceedings*, May, 40–49.

Index